MY AMAZING JOURNEY

DOC YEAGER

AN EXTRAORDINARY LIFE

Book Eight

Dr. Michael H Yeager

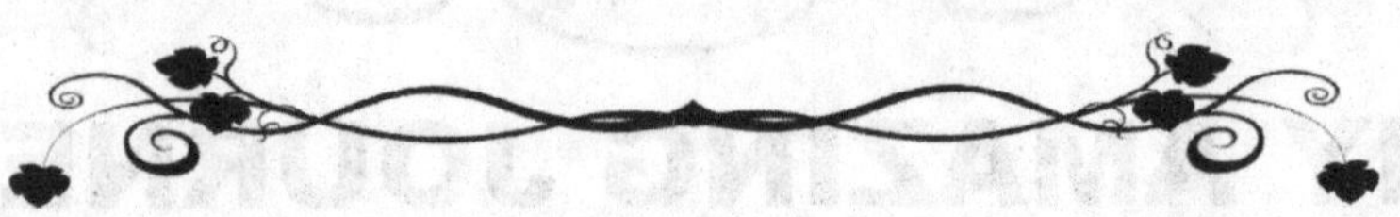

Many of the Names of Those Mentioned in These Books Have Been Changed to Protect the Innocent and the Guilty!

DEDICATION

We dedicate this book to those who are truly hungry and thirsty to live in the realm of the supernatural, and to those who have already tasted of the heavenly realm. We dedicate this to the bride of Christ, those who are called to go deeper, higher, and farther than they have yet experienced. It is only by the grace that comes by FAITH in CHRIST that we will be able to accomplish His will in this earth.

Introduction

Doc Yeager continues his memoirs in the third book. The adventures and experiences he has had, does not diminish, but rather increases. Strap on your seatbelts, and get ready for an amazing journey, true life adventures and experiences. The miraculous happenings, heavenly visitations, and divine deliverance's that you will read in the following books are all true. They have happened personally to my family and me. These experiences are recalled and shared to the best of our ability.

By no means do the following stories account for all the visitations and miracles of God that we have experienced in our lives. If we would recount every single answer to prayer, and every incredible miracle and blessing, there would be no end to this book! Both my wife and I, including our children, have had many supernatural dreams, visions, healings and experiences. In some of our heavenly encounters, God gave us specific information which has happened, as well as visions and dreams which have yet to be fulfilled.

What we are about to share with you in these books are simply highlights of what we have experienced. Some of these experiences will seem to be incredulous; however, they are true. This is not a testimony of how spiritual we are, but how wonderful and marvelous the Father, the Son, and the Holy Ghost are! We share these experiences to the best of our recollections and understanding.

GOD Said: You Better Not Lie or You'll Die!

One day in 1979, I picked up a book by a well-known author. This book had come highly recommended by one of my favorite preachers at that time. The topic was about angelic visitations. This was something I was interested in, because of my many experiences with the supernatural. I began to read this book and noticed immediately that there were experiences he said he had, which did not seem to line up with the Scriptures. I did not want to judge his heart, but we do have the responsibility to examine everything in light of God's Word. If it does not line up with the word of God, then we must reject it, no matter who wrote it.

As I was pondering the stories in this book, the Spirit of the Lord spoke to my heart very strongly. It was as if He was standing right there next to me, speaking audibly. What He spoke to me was rather shocking! The Lord told me that the writer of this book would be dead in three months from a heart attack. I asked the Lord why He was telling me this. He said the stories in the man's book were exaggerated, and that he had opened the door for the devil to steal his life. The Lord warned me that day that if I were ever to do the same thing, judgment would come to me. I did not realize that the Lord would have me to be writing books, many of them filled with my own experiences. Now I know why he spoke this to me, telling me that I better not exaggerate my experiences.

When the Spirit of the Lord spoke this to me, I turned and told my wife. I held the book up and said, in a very quiet whispering, trembling, wavering voice, "Honey, the man who wrote this book will be dead in three months from a heart attack." Plus, I told her why the Lord told me this. I wish I had been wrong. Exactly three months later, the man died from a heart attack. God can speak to us through the positive and the negative circumstances of life. We better take heed to what he is saying.

CONTENTS

ACKNOWLEDGMENTS

*To our heavenly Father and His wonderful love.

*To our Lord, Savior and Master — Jesus Christ, Who saved us and set us free because of His great love for us.

*To the Holy Spirit, Who leads and guides us into the realm of truth and miraculous living every day.

*Thanks to all of those who had a part in helping me get this book ready for publishing.

*To my Lovely Wife, and our precious children, Michael, Daniel, Steven, Stephanie, Catherine Yu, who is our precious daughter-in-law, and Naomi, who is now with the Lord.

CHAPTER ONE

Introduction

As you take this journey with Doc Yeager and his family you will be discovering the good and the bad. The ups and downs. The wonderful and the terrible. Life in this world will always have its successes and its failures. It is the author's desire that you learn along the way. Hopefully you'll discover many truths, secrets, mysteries about what brings Life and death into people's lives.

The Bible itself reveals to us the ups and downs of God's saints. Not only do we discover the life of the saints, but we also discover the lives of others. Even as those within the Scriptures lives were full of trials, tests, tribulations, failures, and victories, so you would discover as you walk these **Memoirs of the Yeager Family.**

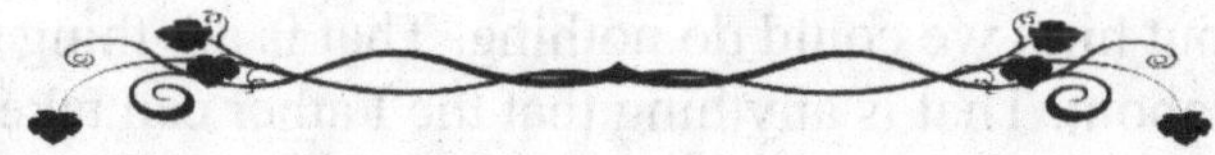

<u>This Book is the School of Hard Knocks</u>

Before I share with you my many Adventures, my family and I have experienced, let's look at the scriptures. As human beings, we are all subject to personal stupidity. Sheep are not very smart at all. I could do a whole book alone on the stupidity of sheep. At one time we had a petting zoo. In this petting zoo, we had close to a dozen sheep. Sheep by nature are not smart. That is why God uses them as an illustration as an example of the believer. Sheep need a shepherd.

They need someone to lead them, guide them, protect them, provide for them, deliver them, and help them survive. Jesus boldly declared that he was the Shepherd of the sheep. Christ Jesus is the brains of the outfit. Throughout eternity, He and He alone will lead us and guide us.

He is the Vine, and we are the dumb branches. (Do we realize that Adam and his wife were sheep before they ever transgressed and sinned against God? The man was created with the absolute need for a shepherd.) Have you ever seen professionally trained sheep?

Men have trained all kinds of animals: dogs, cats, elephants, bears, tigers, etc. The list of animals that men have trained are endless, but do you know one thing we have not seen? Sheep. Do you know why? Because sheep are known to be extremely stupid.

They are the only domesticated animal that cannot live in the wild. Dogs, cats, horses, pigs, birds; almost all domestic animals can live in the wild on their own. Why not sheep? Because sheep need a shepherd!

Now please, do not be offended by this statement. I am not demeaning you or myself. These are simply the facts. Jesus said that without him, we could do nothing. That is anything worthy of speaking about. That is anything that the Father can take pleasure in. We desperately need Jesus in every aspect and dimension of our lives. Listen to what scripture teaches us in the

book of Psalms:
Psalm 119:71 It is good for me that I have been afflicted; that I might learn thy statutes. (Read this Scripture again)

Psalm 119:67 Before I was afflicted I went astray: but now have I kept thy word.   (Did you hear what the psalmist said)

Psalm 94:12 Blessed is the man whom thou chastenest, O Lord, and teachest him out of thy law;13 That thou mayest give him rest from the days of adversity, until the pit be digged for the wicked. (This is a declaration of God working in us)

<u>Please Read This Warning</u>

The Lord had me write these books not to impress you or to cause you to think more or less of me. It is written for the sole purpose of instructing, teaching, revealing how God works behind or in the midst of life events. Also, you can see the demonic world always striving to destroy our lives.

These books are meant to be giving hope to those who seem to be hopeless. It reveals how easily our hearts go astray, and yet God is there. There are many things that we share about God's Divine interventions and HOW we missed God, and yet, in spite of it, He was there. This book is written with the hopes that others will see

#1 Hidden dangers, traps and snares of the enemy.

#2 Where there's hope even in the most hopeless situation.

#3 That we are easily led astray, thereby desperately needing to depend upon God for every decision.

#4 That if we repent, cry out to God, He will hear our feeble pleas and rescue us.

#5 That there are consequences to all of our decisions even though we are forgiven.

#6 If we truly are God's people, the Lord will put us into a melting pot, turn up the heat and cause all of the impurities to come to the surface. Once they manifest, it is up to us what we do with them.

#7 That your heart will even be tested and revealed in the reading of this book.

Many times when bad things happen in our life, the enemy of our soul, the devil, is whispering in our ears that God does not love us. He makes accusations that it is God's fault that these bad things are happening and that the Lord is not faithful to His Word nor His promises. It is time for us to rise up, repent, speak the word, and come against the works of the devil. Yes, Lord, I admit that I am stupid and that I desperately need you more than anything in all of life or creation, "I Need You, Cause I Am Stupid!"

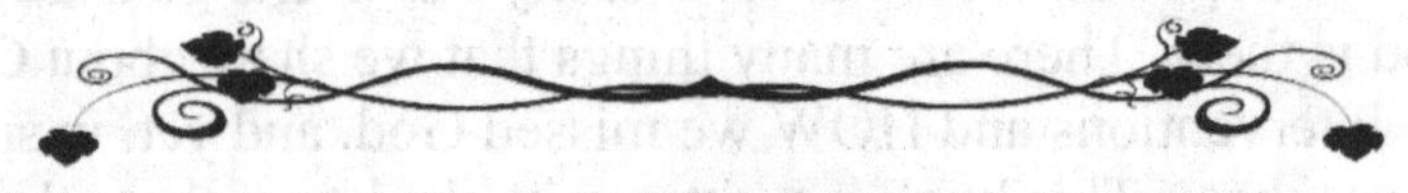

1992

Bought a House before I Saw It

One day I received a phone call from a brother who attended our church. He was in a town about 10 miles from where we lived, working on a demolition job. He informed me that he was working for a man whose house had burned down. The owner of this particular house had received his insurance money and was simply trying to remove some household items before he sold it. As this brother was working for this man it came into his heart that he needed to call me.

He informed me that the house was on a corner lot next to Route 34, in Biglerville Pennsylvania. This gentleman who had received the fire insurance check simply wanted to sell the house the way it was. I asked this brother how much he was asking for it, just out of curiosity, not really wanting any involvement.

He told me that he was selling it for only $12,000 due to the fact the house itself would have to be demolished and removed from the property before it could be used to be rebuilt upon. It was connected to the local sewage system and had a good well on the property.

Up out of my belly came these words: tell the owner of the house that I will buy it the way it is for $12,000. This brother asked me to repeat myself, and I did. He said to me: pastor, you haven't even seen this house. Yes, I know I haven't, but for some reason I am to buy this house.

Tell the owner of the house that it is sold. Now this was strange, because number one, I hadn't seen the house, and number two, I had no money. It just came up out of my heart, and out of my mouth before I knew what I was saying. I knew that this was **GOD**, because I had great peace and joy during this decision and declaration.

Later that day I took a ride over to this house and was pleasantly surprised at its size and condition. I was expecting a house that was almost utterly burned down, and yet I saw that there was the potential for it to be restored to its former glory.

I called up my banker, informing him what I wanted to do. I think that was probably one of the fastest loans I had ever received to purchase this house, with some extra funds to begin work on it. I called up a gentleman who I knew that could begin to strip the house of all the burned and charred wood, including much of the roof. He had a team of men and had a large dump truck, in which he could haul away all the damaged furnishings, including the destroyed parts of the house. This part of the renovation was $12,000.

One day I was at the garage where I always had my vehicles. The owner of this mechanic shop was a wonderful **Spirit** filled brother in **CHRIST**. He was not a member of our church currently. One day as I was picking up a vehicle he had been working on, out of the blue he asked me: did you buy that house located in Biglerville out on route 34?

Yes, I answered him. He told me that him and his wife had just sold their house and were very interested in purchasing this house that I had just bought. I informed him that at this moment there was no plans on selling this house. That we were hoping to fix it up, and possibly rent it out. He told me that they were really interested in that house and asks if I was sure I did not want to sell it. I told him that at this time we were not interested, but I would pray about it.

I went back and told my wife that our mechanic and his wife would like to buy this house that we were having rebuilt. I asked her opinion. She told me that it really did not matter to her, and that I could decide. I did pray about it, having the perception that if we could sell it for a profit, that we should. The next day I went back, informing this brother that I would be willing to sell it.

I told him up front that I had paid $12,000 for the house and invested another 12,000 in it being renovate up to this moment. That I would be willing to sell it for what I had invested plus $30,000 more. This is the figure that had come to my mind as I had prayed about it. To my surprise he immediately agreed to this price. He and his wife would give us $54,000 for a house that we had only had for about a month. Our profit would be $30,000 in one month, which was more money than I made in the year at the church I pastored.

As I was driving back to our house, I literally heard the voice of **GOD** in my heart say to me: what are you going to do with the $30,000 you just made? I said to the Lord: Father you know that everything I have is yours, you tell me what you want me to do with it. He told me specifically that we were to take this $30,000 and give it to the work of the kingdom. Without any hesitation in my heart, I said: okay Lord!

I went back to see this brother in **CHRIST,** informing him what I had heard the Lord say to me. I told him, simply give me $24,000, and make a donation of $30,000 to the work of **GOD**. This is exactly what this couple did. This brother and his wife became active members in our church. They are still friends of ours. And he is still our mechanic. They did fix up this house, which is quite beautiful now. They still live there to this day.

Revelation 4:11 Thou art worthy, O Lord, to receive glory and honour and power: for thou hast created all things, and for thy pleasure they are and were created.

Bought 40 Acres to Build a Community

We discovered that there was 40 acres of land that was for sale right across from our church property. We had already purchased 10 acres on that side of the road. This is where our radio tower for our AM station was situated.

We contacted the owner of this property which was the supervisor for the town of Gettysburg. We came to an agreed-upon price. Our Elders agree to the price and the terms. The owner agreed to give us a certain amount of time to pay him the asking price.

$25,000.00 Logging Operation

A local Minister friend of mine was involved in the logging industry. He told me that if we cut the trees our self that we could pull twice as much from the wood then if we were paid by another Logger who would cut down every tree (clear cut). Plus we would be selective to only cut first grade and second grade trees!

I bought two good chain saws, and we began the project. We would cut the trees down, then cut them in eight feet and six inches.

Veneer Trees/Logs: Typically the highest quality logs, most of which come from the butt log (i.e., the first log above the stump). Most veneer buyers require a minimum veneer log length of 8 ft – 6 inches. The extra 6 inches is for trim allowance.

We dragged these logs out into a clear field where different buyers would come through and make us offers on these logs! They usually will give you a good price on a couple logs then try to rip you off on the others. We only sold the logs that we were given good prices on. By selling our logs that way we really were able to make good money. We were able to pull about $25,000.00 from this project.

We took this money and put it down on the property. During this time, we had begun to draw up plans to build **a refirement center** for retired ministers and those who had been involved in ministry. It was going to consist of single homes, and duplexes. The idea was to keep these Ministers involved in Ministry.

Kathee Has a Head On Collision

As Ron Morris and I were logging the woods across

the highway from our church and the parsonage, my wife was at home with the children. During this time some kind of illness hit my wife. She began to run a very high temperature, became congested and felt miserable.

I would go home to check on her periodically praying for her. She told me that she would be okay and keep on working. One evening when Ron and I was finishing up the day my wife decided to come over and find me. She had finished supper, and it was time to eat. She also had taken sinus medication which was making her a little bit delirious. She jumped into our caravan and headed over.

She pulled into the passing lane on the other side thinking that it was a turning lane. She was trying to figure a way to get over into the woods. She was so caught up in trying to find a way over that she literally pulled in front of another vehicle headed in the opposite direction and was in the passing lane. He saw her coming towards him and slammed on the brakes.

The other gentleman tried to swerve to where he would not hit her head on. Thank **God** when he hit her, he was not going very fast. He did clip my wife's front left fender.

Ron and I heard the crash, and we ran up front to Highway 30 to see what was going on. There my wife was in the vehicle. I opened the door, and she was able to crawl out. She told me that she yeas okay but was still very delirious because of the medication and the sickness. She really wanted to go home bad. It was only about 500 feet to our house. I told her to go home that I would deal with the police.

When the police arrived, I told them exactly what had happened. They were upset because my wife had walked away from the accident, but I told them she was not feeling good at all. By **God's** mercy and grace, they allowed it to slide. **God** has been so good to us through the years when so many times we've could've been killed.

Bought a Pig in a Poker (wet Land)

As we began to prepare the land for the construction by installing roads, the Corps of Engineers stop by. They informed us that a lot of this land was what is called wetland. All of plans for this land came to a complete stop. At that moment it looked like the land had no value. Yet in spite of this land being wetland, eventually it turned out to our benefit, and we sold it for more than what we paid for it in 2007.

Three-year court battle

We contacted the owner telling him the land was useless. That we were going to turn the land back to him. We were not even going to ask to get our money back.

We discovered later that he knew it was wetland before he sold it to us. He told us he wanted his money and did not want the land back. We hired a wetland expert to find out how much of the land was useless.

During this time, we were negotiate with the owner. Eventually he decided to sue us in court to get the money. I had a **Christian** attorney that represented us. I asked her what I should do? She said you're going to have to counter sue him because there was fraud involved.

As I was in prayer over the situation, I heard the Lord told me that this would be a three year trial. It would literally be three years before everything was brought back to where it should be. Sure, enough that is exactly what happened.

Corrupt Town Attorney, Supervisor, Judge

As we began to get involved with the court case, it became obvious that all the officials who were involved were corrupt. Now, we are talking about little Gettysburg Pennsylvania.

I also have discovered in my dealing with the local township supervisors that most of them are also very corrupt. Through the years they have lied to me to my face on numerous occasions. They have made up laws that did not exist to put us under their thumb. In one such situation the lie was so blatant from the Township supervisors that they finally had to acknowledge to me that they had lied.

I do not know why we are so surprised by the

corruption in Washington DC. Most people who seek positions of position and power are not doing it for the people, but for their own selfish and evil purposes. This is even revealed to us in the book of James.

James 2:5 Hearken, my beloved brethren, Hath not God chosen the poor of this world rich in Faith, and heirs of the kingdom which he hath promised to them that love him?6 But ye have despised the poor. Do not rich men oppress you, and draw you before the judgment seats?7 Do not they blaspheme that worthy name by the which ye are called?

As we got ready for trial and begin to do depositions with the opposing attorney, supervisor, I sat in the room just listening to them telling lie after lie. For instance, when we had gone to settlement, I had brought my sister instead of the church's official secretary. According to the law the churches recognized secretary would have to sign the documents. When the seller's attorney discovered that I had not brought the church's secretary he said he could handle it. He filled out official documents and made my sister a temporary secretary for the corporation.

It turns out this was completely illegal. He did not represent us but the sellers. It was a conflict of interest, and from that moment forward none of the documents should have been legal. But I have discovered through the years that those in authority will twist laws, ignore laws, to fulfill whatever it is they desire. As I share this, there is absolutely no bitterness in my heart. I just have a recognition of how wicked and evil the heart really is.

Jeremiah 17:9 The heart is deceitful above all things, and desperately wicked: who can know it?

The seller who was also the head supervisor for Gettysburg Township, lied under oath and said that he did not know what wetland was. And yet we had **evidence** to show that he had been in meetings where they had discussed wetland. Through discovery we also found out that there was a cassette recording with him in the meeting discussing wetlands.

The judge who was to preside over the case was a close friend of the opposing lawyer and supervisor. He would go to different events including baseball games with them. We asked him to recuse himself because of his close ties with these people. He basically scoffed us and refused to the legal precedent.

Recusal, also referred to as judicial disqualification, is the process of a judge stepping down from presiding over a particular case in which the judge may have a conflict of interest.

Another Watergate

During what the court system calls discovery, we subpoenaed the cassette tape which was used to record the meeting at which the seller of the property was in attendance.

The sewage enforcement officer informed our attorneys that for some reason this cassette tape had been erased. Now, I had been recording preaching messages on cassettes for many years, literally thousands, and not once did we ever accidentally erase the tape. You cannot do this accidentally. But this was their excuse.

On that tape would have been explicit information that revealed the seller knew exactly what wetland was. He knowingly and willingly sold land to the church without telling us it was wetland. Yet the laws very specific that you must let the buyer aware if there's any problems with the real estate, specifically environmental issues. This reminds me very much of what happened with Nixon and Watergate.

The missing 18 1/2 minutes: Presidential destruction of incriminating evidence.

The Nixon White House tapes are audio recordings of conversations between U.S. President Richard Nixon and Nixon administration officials, Nixon family members, and White House staff, produced between 1971 and 1973.[1]

On November 17, 1973, the White House informed Federal District Judge John Sirica that the 18 1/2 minute Nixon-Haldeman conversation of June 20, 1972, had been erased. White House Counsel Fred Buzhardt told the Court that he no explanation for the erasure.

CHAPTER TWO
Called Me a TV Evangelist

There's a lot of water under the bridge during the three years that we were going to this court case. I experienced much ridicule and mockery from those in positions of power within the government. One day I was sitting in the court, and they began to call me a telly evangelist. Now, it is true that I was on TV, but I was no telly evangelist.

I knew in my heart why they were doing this. It was a derogatory term, and this was during the time of Jim Baker who was arrested and imprisoned. It was also during the time of the scandals of Larry Lee, and Bob Tilton. They basically were painting me with a negative image so that when I had a jury trial, they would all look down on me.

They were discussing what a telly evangelist is, so I stood up and I told the judge that I was a pastor and not a telly evangelist. He told me to shut up and sit down. Later on he did apologize because it turns out I had a right to defend myself. But this is the kind of abuse that I had to endure throughout these three years of this court case.

Realized We would Lose in Court

The day had come for the trial to begin. The jury was picked. Everybody was seated where they needed to be. As I was praying, I looked over at the jury, and my heart fell. Somehow, they had picked people who seem to be antagonistic against ministers. I literally could see venom and hate radiating from their faces.

I knew within my heart of hearts at that moment that I was not going to win this court case. Even though we should've easily won because of the lies and deceptions that were used to get us to buy this property, they were going to twist the facts.

We had already spent close to $50,000 with everything involved in this court case. The only ones that were going to make out, where the attorneys. And if we appealed the case if we lost it, it would be another 60 $70,000. I called my attorney over to me. I said to her let's make an offer to settle this. She agreed with me wholeheartedly.

Our attorney went over and spoke to their attorney, then who spoke to the seller. Within 1/2 an hour we came to a place of agreement. We were just going to have to swallow the sour pill and **Believe God** to come up with the money to pay for land that at this moment seem useless.

I'm glad to say years later we sold the land for five times the amount that we paid for. Of course, we did not hide the fact that there was environmental issues. Yet the buyers, purchased it as a future investment.

Local Newspaper Lies about Our Church

As a final note there were other issues involved in our local community. The local newspaper took up a crusade against us. They wrote an article about us painting us as if we were some kind of cult.

Lie after lie was in the newspaper. During this time my sister Debbie who had been my secretary, decided to move back to Wisconsin. The newspaper stated that I had left the ministry. Immediately when this newspaper article was released our phone began to ring off the hook.

Here our congregation thought that I had left and basically was running for my life. We never did recover from that damage that the newspaper article ran. Somehow it made it sound like we had taken financial advantage of the congregation. It made it sound like I had ran away with all the money. Which was ridiculous because we were operating week by week financially.

We did get a hold of the newspaper company, but they did not want to talk to us. We told them that they needed to retract their article. We asked them how come they never contacted us before they wrote this article? They never responded to the question!

They did put a very small notice in the very back of their paper stating that pastor Michael H Yeager was still with the congregation at **Jesus** Is Lord Ministries International.

Pastors Come to Our Rescue

When this slanderous newspaper article came out About **Jesus** Is Lord Ministries International, four full gospel pastors in our local community stood up for the church. These are four pastors that I would go out and eat with usually once a month.

They got together and wrote an article to the local newspaper. They stated that it was amazing that they had not done more investigation before they brought out their negative response to the church and its court case. They mentioned that the newspaper never responded or reported to all the good works the local church was involved with. Taking care of the homeless, feeding the hungry, ministry to the prison personnel. Plus many other activities that the church had done through the years for the local community.

The newspaper did print this article but right below it they attacked the pastors. They said this article was not about the church's good deeds though they may be many, but about the ongoing court case.

Of course, the newspaper's original article was not really about the court case, it was just basically a slanderous attack, based upon false information against the church and his congregation.

Typical Missionary Journey

I arrived in the Philippines with some kind of stomach flu, or virus, and I became deathly sick. On top of the sickness, I was extremely tired because of jet lag. The trip over was a nightmare! I had used a foreign airline to get a low price, but you get what you pay for. It was a crowded flight, with babies crying and filling their diapers.

The air in the airplane was extremely hot and stuffy; it stunk so bad that I almost had to breathe through my shirt. The seats on the plane were very small and uncomfortable.

The person sitting next to me was practically sitting on my lap! The journey was almost twenty-four hours long. When I arrived in Manila, I had to catch another small plane which would take me to the province of Samar, to the town of Calbayog City.

I waited about four hours before I boarded the small plane to get to Calbayog. When I landed at the airport in Calbayog, I had to take what they call a Jeepney, which looks like a Willies Jeep, only it's about ten times bigger. I had to ride this Jeep, crowded with other travelers, all the way out to where I was to meet up with the **Believers** I was working with.

There are no windows in the Jeepney - except for the very front windshield. Because of this, I breathed in diesel fuel for hours while traveling on rough, bouncy roads. Filipinos were pushing up against me all the way. I felt like an animal crowded in a cage.

After more than thirty hours without sleep my head was throbbing so bad I could hardly handle it. I felt like I was going to pass out at any minute. I was sicker then sick. Finally, after what felt like a never-ending nightmare, I arrived at Catarman, where I was scheduled to preach. In the natural, I was in no condition to preach or minister. Yet, I made it to my first meeting. The building had a tin roof, walls made of block, and the seats were wooden benches with no backs.

I almost fell over, right then and there, but I buckled down and gritted my teeth. When it was time for me to speak, the **Spirit** of **GOD** quickened my mortal flesh.

I preached like a house on fire! For the next twenty days, nonstop, I preached every chance they gave me. My mind, heart, and body were energized and quickened by the **Holy Ghost**. This is the life of **Violent Faith**!

James 1:2-4 My brethren, count it all joy when ye fall into divers temptations; 3 Knowing this, that the trying of your Faith worketh patience. 4 But let patience have her perfect work, that ye may be perfect and entire, wanting nothing.

A Brief Description of Faith:
When GOD, His Word and His will are Supernaturally Quickened to you by the Holy Spirit! These realities become more real to you than anything in life. It is a revelation of who JESUS CHRIST & GOD, the Father really are!

What they have done and are doing. It is a quickening in your heart, when you know, that you know, that you know, that you know: if GOD is with you, then who can be against you?
CHRIST JESUS, Himself, lives inside of you. Your mind, your will, your emotions, and every part of your being is overwhelmed with the reality of JESUS CHRIST! And you enter the realm where all things are possible! This is where, by God's grace, it is my hope and desire to take you.

Offered Prostitute, Philippines

As I was going to the Philippines there were times when I had to stop off at a hotel. Of course the hotels in the Philippines are nothing compared to the hotels in America. When I landed in Manila I had about a five hour to eight hour wait to catch the small prop plane out to the province of Samar.

I asked someone where there was a cheap hotel close by for I could get a little bit of sleep, it had been 24 hours since I had left home. The Filipino airline that I had taken was extremely cramped. The whole trip was more like a nightmare than anything else. Someone told me about a local hotel, and I flagged a taxi. When I arrived at this rundown motor Lodge I went to the office. I told them I only wanted a room for about 5 to 6 hours to get some sleep.

We agreed upon a certain price, and they gave me the keys to the room. As I walked into the room there were mirrors that were hanging from the ceilings in the walls. Also, there was strange steel contraptions. Of course, a new that this was all designed to be a place of fornication and adultery. I ignored all of this foolishness and took a quick shower. As I was getting ready to take a much-needed sleep there was a knock on my door.

I opened up the door very precociously and there was a Filipino man who was probably about 40 who was standing there. I asked him what he wanted? He said to me in broken English: do you want a woman? I said: What? He said to me again: do you want a woman? I responded by telling him that I was a happily married man. That I was also a minister of the gospel.

It is like he did not hear a word I said so the next thing he said was even more disgusting. He said: do you want a young boy? I told him I did not want a young boy or a woman! I was beginning to get upset with him because I was tired and I wanted to get some sleep, plus this was all sick and perverted. Then he said to me: do you want a young girl? Now I was really upset. I began to preach **Jesus Christ** to him in a very bold way. When I got done he just stared at me.

Then he said this: I am a **Christian** also, but I need to make a living, and this is how I make my living. I was not going to argue with this foolishness, so I just simply closed the door in his face. I locked the bolts on the door. Then I slid the chain that was attached to the metal frame to the door. I crawled into bed and fell fast asleep.

I woke up just in time to call for a cab. I got into the cab and headed to the airport. That's the last time I ever went to that motel on my trips to the Philippines.

He Was Going to Get US KILLED

We had been ministering in the province of Samar. While we were there, a minister from Manila had been attending some of our pastor conferences. In the conference, I had simply stated that we were not afraid to die for the gospel. Whether it be by the Communists or any other physical or natural disaster, nothing would stop us from doing **God's** will. This particular pastor seemed to be enamored with the thought that we were not afraid of the Communists. That wasn't our message. We were not there to challenge the Communists or to Americanize the Philippine nation and its people. We were there to preach the gospel of **JESUS CHRIST**.

Because we needed to contact the airline three days in advance before we were to leave, we had to have someone in Manila let them know the date we were leaving. Our tickets were open ended, meaning we could leave anytime we wanted to, we just had to let them know three days in advance. This particular minister, who seemed to be enamored with our lack of fear, was headed back to Manila. We asked him if he would please let the airlines know when we were going to be leaving. He said he would be glad to do that for us. We gave him the dates that we were leaving.

There was unrest in my soul as we said goodbye to him. There was just something about him that made me extremely hesitant to **Trust** him. When we were finished with our meetings in Samar, we caught a plane ride back to Manila. We called this minister, and he came and picked us up in his car at the airport. When we got into his vehicle, he began to talk right away about the meetings he had lined up for us. I asked him, "What meetings are you talking about? We are to be leaving tomorrow." I asked him whether or not he had contacted the airlines for us. He informed us in a hesitant murmuring way that he had not.

The red lights began to flash in my heart right away. It's like I heard the Lord say, get on a plane tomorrow, and get out of this nation. This man has set you up to be murdered. I leaned over and told my friend what the **Spirit** had spoken to me. He agreed with me one hundred percent. I told him that we were sorry, but that we could not accommodate him since we were leaving the next day.

He looked back at us, and basically said that's impossible. You have to give a three-day notice. You might as well go ahead and minister at the meetings I have set up. We discovered later that he had been making outrageous statements about us, making it sound like we were there to challenge the Communists and were not afraid to die. Of course, the NPA would come to kill us, not because we were preaching **JESUS CHRIST,** but because this man made it sound like we were challenging them and their movement. I did not argue with this man any longer. We stayed at his house that night.

Early in the morning, we woke up and got ready to go to the airport. We discovered he had not taken us seriously about taking us to catch a flight. We insisted that he take us immediately. Finally, he grudgingly agreed. We had him drop us off at the airport and told him he could go home. He said he would wait for us because he knew it was impossible for us to leave. We went to the main office of the airline.

They informed us that our tickets could not be changed because we were flying economy and their plane had already been booked to capacity for the day. I very politely asked if there was someone higher up we could speak to. He took us to a gentleman. We explained to him we needed to leave. When he asked why, I informed him we could not give him a direct answer to his question, but we simply needed to leave. He asked us to wait a little bit for an answer. We stepped out of his office into the foyer.

After a little while, he called us back in. He told us that they were going to do it. Amazingly, they had bought us tickets from a much more expensive airline. He handed us two new tickets and told us that we better hurry to catch the flight, which was boarding at that very moment. As we ran to catch a flight, we saw the minister standing behind the rope line waiting for us. We waved goodbye to him as we headed to catch our flight home.

I know thy works: behold, I have set before thee an open door, and no man can shut it: for thou hast a little strength, and hast kept my word, and hast not denied my name (Revelation 3:8).

CHAPTER THREE

GOD Asked Me: Will You Die for Me?

I heard the voice of **GOD** asking me: are you willing to die for me? It was as I was getting ready to leave for the Philippines. I had been to the Philippines on numerous occasions. I had been going into an area of the Philippines where the NPA was extremely active. NPA is the abbreviation for the new People's Army, which are part of a communist movement.

At that time, they were very active, and they were extremely brutal and dangerous. **God**ly men which I have worked with in the Philippines had been murdered by them. I heard the Lord continue to say to me: if I can use your spilt blood like a seed planted into the ground to bring about a wonderful harvest, are you willing to die? When I heard the Lord say this to me, I took it very

29

seriously. With deep sorrow in my heart and tears rolling down my face, I said yes Lord!

It was not that I was not willing to die for **CHRIST,** because I had been in many dangerous situations since I had been born again in 1975. I have had numerous encounters with people threatening and trying to kill me. A gang I used to run with out of Chicago tried twice.

Some Yupik Indians in Alaska had tried to kill me. A demon possessed woman had stabbed me multiple times in the face and yet the knife could not penetrate my skin. A Gang leader in Chicago tried stabbing me to death, the shot me with a shot gun, (but nothing happened) A radical Muslim kept on wanting to shoot me, as he yelled and screamed in my face, with his finger ready to pull the trigger which would have sent me off into eternity, but the **Holy Ghost** restrained him.

Yes, I was more than willing to die, but in truth I did not want to. I had a lovely wife, 3 sons and a beautiful little girl. But I said yes Lord, if this is your will! I still remember that morning as I was getting ready to drive myself to the BWI Airport to catch a plane to the Philippines.

I hugged my precious wife very tight and my four beautiful children as if it was like the last time, I would ever hold them or hug them again on this side of heaven. As I looked at my little girl Stephanie, she was sucking on her 2 fingers, and I had lovingly nicknamed her two fingers Stephanie. My 2nd son Daniel, I had nicknamed him the watermelon kid because he loved watermelon so much. I hugged my oldest son goodbye who we had nicknamed Mick which is short for Michael. my 3rd son Steven could never give enough hugs even to this day.

As I backed out of my driveway leaving my family standing on the front porch tears were rolling down my face. I said Lord you died for me, you gave everything for me, so the least I can do is to be willing to give up everything you've given me, if I can be a seed of revival for others to be born again. As I was driving towards the airport on the main highway, I was weeping so hard that I could barely see where I was going.

I was thanking **GOD** for the years that he had given me with my lovely wife Kathleen. I was thanking **GOD** for my 3 sons and my daughter. I was thanking **GOD** for all the opportunities he had given to me to minister the word and help others. I was also reflecting upon the fact of how many times I should been dead like many of my former buddies who were now dead.

I thought back on the times before I was born again when I had overdosed, drank way too much booze, played chicken with oncoming trains, driving on the other side of the road headed right towards others. When I had been in a gunfight with a crazy man. Oh, how many times **GOD** had spared me, and yet most of my worldly friends were now dead.

All those times when **GOD** spared my life, he could've allowed me to die and go to hell. But **GOD** had rescued me, and now it was my turn to die for him, how could I say no? I remember landing in the Philippines. I was completely free from fear. In my heart of hearts, I was already a martyr for **CHRIST**.

Now to my wonderful amazement and my great surprise **GOD** spoke to my heart while I was over there in the communist infested area. **He said: son you're not going to die!** I said what Lord? **He spoke to me again: you're not going to die!** I remember crying with joy, I said why Lord?

He said I needed to have you prove your love for me. He said I needed to have you to know that I was number 1 in your life. Even as Abraham offered up Isaac, and I gave him back, so in a sense you have offered up your wife and your children, and I give them back to you.

That has been over 25 years ago when the Lord spared my life. I'm still going to areas at times that are extremely dangerous, but I have no fear, because I know that **GOD** is with me. What if he ever asked me to offer up my life again as a seed with the shedding of my blood? All I can say is that if it ever happens again, by **God's** grace I'll say, yes Lord! You gave your life for me, it's the least I can do.

Be ye angry, and sin not: let not the sun go down upon your wrath: Neither give place to the devil (Ephesians 4:26-27).

Into the Mountains with a Motorcycle

Now I had earned a reputation for being pretty good on a motorcycle. I really wasn't very good, but the **Spirit** of **GOD** would quicken me when I would take a motorcycle into the mountains to preach in between Crusades and conferences. I'm kind of hyperactive, so when everyone else took a siesta, I would find someone who could interpret for me and head into the mountains.

Driving A Motorcycle at Night Through Communist Infested Area under the Influence of The Holy Ghost!

AN AMAZING TRUE STORY OF ONE OF MY ADVENTURES ON A MOTORCYCLE!

WE WERE TOSSED INTO THE VELVET BLACKNESS OF THE NIGHT AS WE HIT AN ALMOST VERTICAL HUGE PILE OF GRAVEL! WE FOUND OURSELVES WAY ABOVE THE GROUND ON A MOTORCYCLE IN THE UTTER BLACKNESS OF NIGHT!

To tell this story in it's the proper setting I need to give you some background information. I had been to the Philippines multiple times reaching out to the indigenous people.

The areas I went were considered to be one of the most primitive and dangerous settings in the nation. When I go to the Philippines, I always worked directly with a Filipino Bible college in the province of Samar. I have been told that Samar is one of the most poverty-stricken parts of the Philippines and one of the most dangerous. Missionaries very rarely go there because of this. It is far away from all the modern conveniences of Manila. It is also inhabited by the New People's Army which is a Communist movement. The NPA are extremely dangerous.

I have personally known Philippine pastors who I have ministered with who have been killed by them. During my time in the Philippines, the natives have allowed me to use their motorcycles to go up into the mountains to preach to churches in the boondocks'.

On one of my missionary endeavors, I was just finishing three weeks worst of outreach when the **Spirit** of **God** quickened my heart to ask them a strange question. I said to them: Where it is the most dangerous place to go to in this province? They told me it was an island called Laoang. I asked him why?

They told me that two American missionaries had gone to the island of Laoang, and had not come out alive. The NPA had slit their throats as they were there. There had been no missionary endeavor there for at least 10 years.

As they told me this story, I heard myself say out of the blue: that I needed to go and take this place for **Jesus**. As I declared this bold statement to them, there was an amazing peace within my heart!

I informed them that the next time that I came back to the Philippines, that I needed to go to that island and preach the gospel. They asked me if I was serious. I said absolutely! I told them I would give them the money that they needed to make the flyers and posters to spread the word that we were coming.

Before I left, I was true to my word, and I gave them the money that was necessary to print flyers to distribute to inhabitants of the island.

About six months later, I arrived back in the Philippines with one of the men from my church who is now a pastor in the Phoenix, Arizona area.

When we arrived in the province of Samar, the brethren informed us that the Communists were aware of us coming and were going to be waiting for us. I did not ask them to explain to me what they meant. I absolutely had no fear in my heart. It is hard to explain to people what it is like when you are operating in a gift of **Faith**. It is not normal **Faith**.

It is **Faith** that makes you know that in **Christ** you cannot be defeated. In the operation of this **Faith**, there is always overwhelming peace. It is the peace of **God** that passes all understanding.

The minute you lose your peace, you need to stop and asked the Father what is wrong.

This is a major way in which God leads and guides us is by his peace.

Isaiah 55:12 For ye shall go out with joy, and be led forth with peace: the mountains and the hills shall break forth before you into singing, and all the trees of the field shall clap their hands.

In order to get to this island, we were first going to have to go by land on a worn out concrete road that had been built right after World War II. We had to travel from Catbalogan City to the town of Catarman . Then from Catarman, we continued our journey another 40 miles to reach our canoes that were going to take us to the island. Altogether the journey was hundred and 14 miles. Now, this may not sound like a long-distance when it comes to traveling in America, but that is a long way on a rough Filipino road. We finally reached a river called the Pambujan River.

To our dismay, the bridge was out. They were putting in a brand-new bridge which they had only begun. So we had to take a long alternative route to reach another bridge to get across this river.

This river was over 300 feet wide. (I only mention this because it's an important part of my journey on the motorcycle) We stayed on this road until it ran into the Philippine ocean.

From there we took two large canoes. Each canoe had an outboard motor on the back of them. We would have to traverse on the ocean over a mile to reach Laoang.

After all our equipment and the people were loaded into the first canoe, I found myself up front at the very tip of the vessel. During this time there was great excitement and peace in my heart to see what **God** was about to do.

I was optimistic of **God** manifesting himself on this island that had been shut off from the gospel for many years. I knew that **God** was going to have to perform miracles to keep us alive, and yet there was absolutely no fear within my heart, nothing but overflowing peace.

As we were coming closer to the island, I could see that there were men lined up along the beach waiting for us. There was absolutely no fear in my heart as we approach the island. There were approximately 30 men who were standing there with guns and machetes in their hands.

The Filipino brothers who were navigating the canoes kept the engines of the canoes running fast enough so the canoes would drive themselves up a little bit onto the dry shore. As we approached the shore, I was so excited that I stood up to my feet, getting ready to leap out of this canoe towards these communists. It had to be the **Spirit** of **God** with in me because no sane man would leap to his death. I almost felt like George Washington's famous painting of him crossing the Delaware River.

The moment we hit the beach, I was up and out of that canoe.

The Communists were standing there waiting to kill us. The **Spirit** of **God**, the gift of **Faith**, the peace of **God** was possessing me as I began to walk towards them very rapidly. I headed right for the center of this crowd of gun toting and machete-wielding communist.

As I reached them, something supernatural happened. It was like the Lord splitting the Red Sea, but instead of water, it was men who had murder in their hearts. They separated from left to right and allowed our team of men to walk right through the midst of them.

We Held Our Meeting That Night!

That night we held a crusade right in the middle of the village. As our worship team was singing, the Communists and pagan religious people were marching through our meeting trying to disturb what **God** was doing. We simply ignored them and kept on with the meeting.

There was a very large crowd that night, probably because they wanted to see a white man. It was very seldom when Americans or Europeans came into this area. The tourists flock to Manila yend Mindanao.

It had been 10 years since anybody missionary had even dared come to this island to preach **Christian**ity. The last missionaries that had come they had murdered. Now here I was about to preach the gospel of **Jesus Christ** to them. A message that saves, heals and delivers just like it did in the days when **Jesus** walked in his earthly ministry.

After the singing had been finished, it was my opportunity to preach. It literally felt like the **Spirit** of **God** was flowing through me like a mighty river of electricity and power. I preached under the unction of the **Holy Ghost**, not thinking at all what to say, but letting the **Spirit** have his way. When I was done preaching, there was barely enough light to make out the crowd in front of us.

They had lit some torches around the meeting area, trying to give as much light as possible. Because I could not get down into the crowd to pray for them, I had to speak the word of healing and salvation over them.

I began to command their bodies to be healed in the name of **Jesus Christ** of Nazareth. Every time I would speak something in the name of **Jesus**, the interpreter would translate me into their language.

Miracles began to happen the moment I said: In the Name of **Jesus**. One old lady who had been blind in one eye could now see.

A little boy who had been deaf could now hear. It was too dark out for us to tell how many miracles happened that night, but to this day I have been told there is a thriving church there because of this meeting.

After this large meeting, we were led to a two-story shack. The precious brothers we worked with had made arrangements for us to be put into a two-story house. We would be on the second floor, while they were going to be on the first floor. I know why they did this! They were going to make the Communists have to kill them before they would let the NPA get to us. These were the kind of men that would give their lives without hesitation for the sake of the gospel.

It was late by the time we went to bed. They gave my friend and I some type of straw mats to lie on. We threw these mats on the wooden floor and tried to go to sleep.

During the night, we could hear the Communists outside making a racket. The communist had surrounded our house with groups of men.

They had started little bonfires around the house where we were staying as the communist sat or stood by their fires.

As I went to sleep that night, I saw two large angels like pillars of fire in a dream with swords drawn standing over the top of the house we were staying in. When we woke up in the morning, it was very peaceful. And the Communists were gone.

Time Came to a Standstill as I was Supernaturally empowered to drive a motorcycle through communist infested lands.

Driving Motorcycle under the Influence of The **Holy Ghost**!

We had left the island in the morning, and we were now holding meetings in a town called Pambujan, which was about 19 miles away. **God** was moving in a wonderful way. The Philippine brother who was over all of the work in this area is named Danny. He also had two other brothers, Jonathan and Hurley, who are also ministers of the gospel. (You can friend them on Facebook if you like).

I personally knew their **Father**, Reese Monte's (who has since gone home to be with the Lord), who was an amazing apostle of **God** who was instrumental in starting over five hundred churches throughout the Philippines islands.

The name of the organization was "Faith Tabernacle. These men are all apostolic in nature. If I understand correctly, Danny has been instrumental in starting over seventy churches. Now here I was ministering with Danny. Danny came to me late one night and said he was homesick. He had never been away from his wife this long. We were approximately 32 miles from his home in Catarman.

This may not sound like a long-distance to you, but Believe me, with the road conditions, the weather, and the communist, it was quite a distance, especially if you are going to travel at night. Actually, in this area, I never saw any vehicles out on the road after the sunset.

Now I had earned a reputation for being good on a motorcycle. In all reality, though, I wasn't very good on a motorcycle at all. It is simply that the **Spirit** of **God** would quicken me as I would take a motorcycle up into the mountains to preach the gospel to the natives.

I'm kind of hyperactive, so in between Crusades and conferences. When everyone else was taking a siesta, I would find someone who was willing to go with me to interpret for me, and I would head up into the mountains.

We were deep into a heavily populated area where there were known to be anti-government radicals, Communists, the NPA, and it was extremely dangerous to be there and especially at night. One night, Brother Danny came to me asking me if I would be willing to take him home on a motorcycle that someone had driven who was on our team.

It was a very rainy and foggy night. Now the motorcycle that was available was an old machine—I Believe it was a Kawasaki 250. This motorcycle had some major issues though. The headlights were very dim, and at **Times** the shifting mechanism would fall off if you were not careful.

When Pastor Danny asked me to take him home, the **Spirit** of **God** quickened my heart and said: take him. It was like when David had said he was thirsty for the waters of the well in Bethlehem. Three of his mighty men broke through the host of the Philistines and drew water out of the well in Bethlehem for David to drink. This quickening in my heart was so strong that I told Danny I would take him home to see his precious wife and children without any hesitation.

Danny informed me with almost a whisper that we must not stop along the way no matter what because the Communists would be out in full force. He also said we would have to be very careful because the Communists (if they heard us coming) would stretch a thin cable wire across the road to kill us. I saw a video one **Time** where this is exactly what they had done, and it was captured on film. The motorcyclist was cut right in half. It was not a very pretty site.

Danny also informed me that if they got their hands on us, we would be dead men. Even with this dire warning from Daniel, I had total and perfect peace. Actually, there was a divine excitement within my heart to go on this epic journey. This is not something you can explain to a person who has never experienced the quickening, moving, empowering presence of the **Holy Ghost**. I perceived by the **Spirit** of **God** that a gift of Faith was operating in my heart.

As we began this journey, we had made one major mistake. We forgot that there was road construction all along the way and that the main bridge was out. If we would have remembered, then we have taken a long way around. As it was, we took the regular route that should have been the shortest route to Danny's home Village.

Now, as I was driving the motorcycle, I could barely see where I was going. The rain and the fog were covering the shield of my helmet. The headlight was very dim, almost nonexistent. I had to keep reaching up with my left hand to wipe my face shield to see where I was going. Danny was sitting behind me, holding on tight as I was driving. I Believe I was driving at approximately forty-five to fifty miles an hour.

After we had been on this rough construction road for several miles, I thought that I could see something very dark and threatening in the pathway ahead of us. In my mind, it seemed to me to be an enemy waiting to catch us, and yet I had total peace. I should have slowed down, but I just kept ongoing. The next thing I knew, Danny was yelling very loud in my ear with a great warning, "watch out."

I yelled back at Danny: Hold on, we are going to go through it! Whatever this object was, we slammed into it, doing about 50 miles an hour. As it turned out, it was a very large pile of gravel and road material.

We hit this very large pile of construction material which was almost vertically straight up. The bike, without hesitation, raced to the top of this pile of construction material and launched us up into the void of the night. During this event, Danny took his head and put it underneath my left forearm, under my armpit.

It turns out he had been in a terrible motorcycle accident before, and now he was trying to protect himself as much as he could from the disaster which was unfolding. In every scenario, this was going to be a major catastrophe. Not only would we be killed or extremely hurt when we hit the concrete road, but then the communist would be upon us. No hospitals or help would be available for us. We Surely Were Dead Men!

Here we were launched up into the darkness of the night. As I was up in the air on the back of this motorcycle, it truly felt like I was just sailing through the sky like when I used to fly airplanes. During this experience, I was supernaturally engulfed in an amazing bubble of peace and joy. I had absolutely no fear or anxiety whatsoever. I was operating in the REALM of the **Spirit**ual. Not only where we suspended in the heavens, but **Time** itself has ceased to exist. It seemed like I was in velvet darkness for over an hour. It seemed like for the longest **Time** we were not ever going to come back down.

We were suspended in the heavens. Of course, we must've been sailing through the sky in an upward and downward flow. Obviously, when we hit the wet concrete roadway below us, something would have to give. But when we make contact with the road, it was so smooth, so nonresistant, that it almost felt like putting on a pair of comfortable old bedroom slippers. This is the only way I can describe it. We did not skid, bounce, or slide in any sense of the word.

When we met the road, the only negative thing that happened was that the gear shifter fell off the motorcycle. We were stuck in the Top Gear of the motorcycle as we headed down the road. We had to stop and go back and look for it. We went back to the pile of gravel we had hit and started from the pile, working our way out in order to find the shifter.

I did not think to measure the distance of our jump. But it sure seemed to take a long **Time** to get back to that pile of the road material. We looked and looked and looked with the dim headlight of the motorcycle.

By this **Time**, Danny was very concerned about the Communists seeing the headlight of the motorcycle and hearing its engine running, so we decided to leave the motorbike in top gear and leave. As we were headed down the road at about four hundred feet away from the pile of road gravel, I saw something gleaming on the road in front of us in the rain.

We stopped, and there was the shifting mechanism! We put it back on the bike and went our way. How far we flew through the night sky that night, only **God** Knows! Now, if you think this sounds incredulous, wait until ye hear about the next part of this journey. Pastor Danny Monte's can verify every bit of this journey. He has a Facebook page in the Philippines, in the province of Samara. He can verify every part of this story.

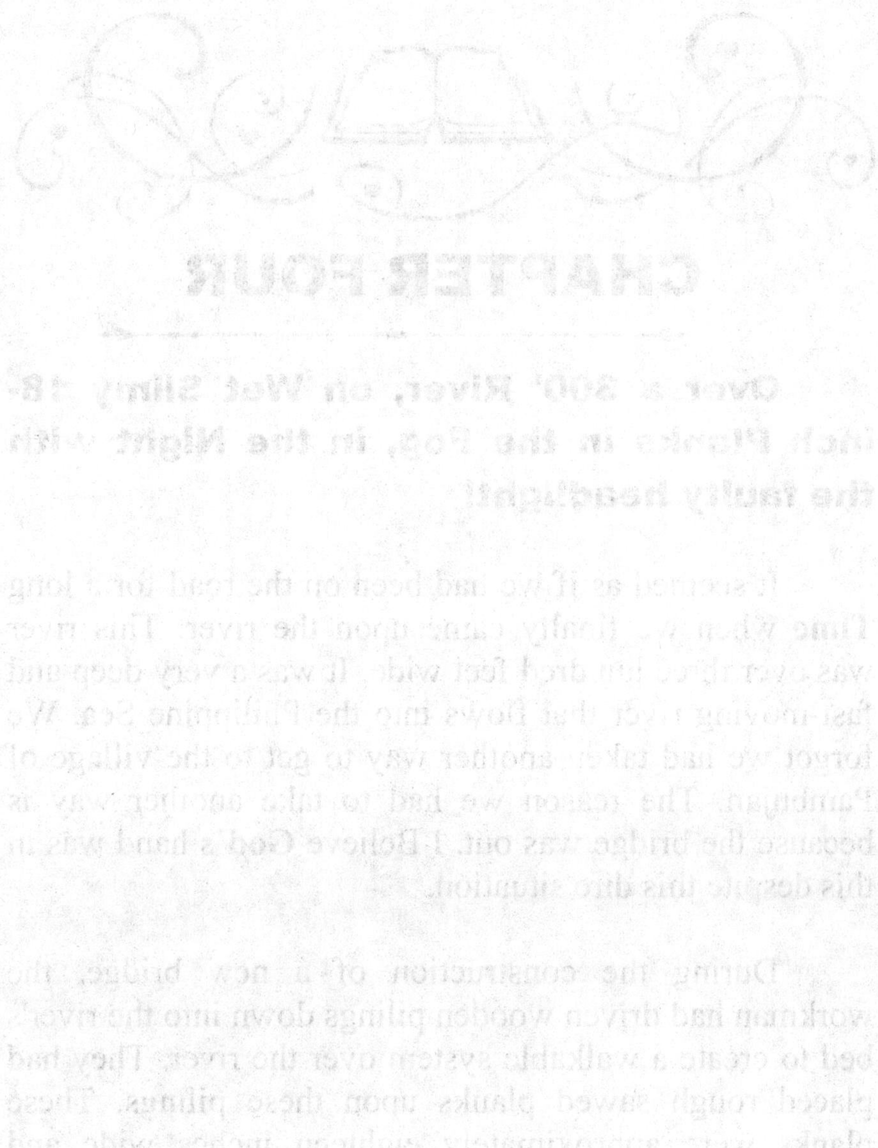

CHAPTER FOUR

Over a 300' River, on Wet Slimy 18-inch Planks in the Fog, in the Night with the faulty headlight!

It seemed as if we had been on the road for a long **Time** when we finally came upon the river. This river was over three hundred feet wide. It was a very deep and fast-moving river that flows into the Philippine Sea. We forgot we had taken another way to get to the village of Pambujan. The reason we had to take another way is because the bridge was out. I Believe **God**'s hand was in this despite this dire situation.

During the construction of a new bridge, the workman had driven wooden pilings down into the river's bed to create a walkable system over the river. They had placed rough sawed planks upon these pilings. These planks were approximately eighteen inches wide and were loosely attached on these pilings.

This footbridge appeared to be four to five feet above the river. These planks were extremely wet and slimy. I would not have wanted to walk on them in the daylight, let alone on a wet and extremely foggy night. To get to the beginning of the planks, you had to go down a muddy embankment and back up a pile of dirt to get to the plank walk bridge. There was no way we could walk that motorcycle across this river.

When we found ourselves in this situation, Danny said to me: "What are we going to do?" The **Spirit** of **God** rose up in me by the gift of faith, and I heard myself say "Hold on, Danny!" When I hit the first plank of approximately 30 planks with my motorcycle's front tire, I shifted into second gear. I watched as our bike sailed across the wet slimy plank in front of me. I gunned the throttle as I continued to drive the motorcycle over the wet, slimy, loose planks—not slipping one **Time**.

If we would have gone to the left or to the right either way, we would have plummeted into the raging river, swallowed up into its strong current, never to be seen or heard of again. It was the **Spirit** of **God** that took us across that three-hundred-foot river in the rain and fog, over slimy wet 18-inch planks, over a precarious bridge that was only made for foot traffic during the daylight.

I'm telling you that if I had not been there to experience this myself, I most likely would not Believe this story. We sailed across that makeshift bridge all the way to the other side without one mistake or mishap. To make a long story short, the Lord saw us safely to Danny's village and house to his wonderful wife and children.

Years later I went on the internet to look at this river that we had crossed. The internet image had been updated in 2010. The new bridge that they were just getting ready to build at that **Time** had been completed. You can see the alternative road we had to take another route until the new bridge had been built. I am overwhelmed at the amazing things I have watched **God** do.

Dangerous Attack of Conjunctivitis!

I am sharing this story in order to help you to understand how to take a hold of your healing. You see John 10:10 says that the thief comes to steal, kill and destroy. It tells us in the book of James to submit ourselves to **GOD**, resist the devil, and he will flee from us. The very minute that any type of physical affliction attack our bodies is the very moment that we need to take a hold of **GOD**, and then come against the enemy of our souls. *Our bodies are the temples of the Holy Ghost, and the enemy has no right to afflict them.*

One of the brothers of the church where I pastor went with me to the Philippines. We were ministering in the province of Samar, which is one of the five provinces of the Philippines. It takes an airplane ride from Manila, and then transferring to ground vehicles. The trip is rather long, tiring and challenging. Not including the fact that we are in the territory of the New People's Army, which is an anti-government communist movement. **Believe** me when I tell you that they will kill you in a heartbeat.

When we finally arrived at our destination, the Filipinos we were working with were waiting for us. The local pastors and **Believers** had already prepared the way for us to hold crusades in different towns and villages. In the natural they really did not need us because they are all walking in the realities of **GOD**. To some extent we Americans are like White Elephants in that we draw a crowd. We do not have any more of the Holy **Spirit** or the word of **GOD** than they do.

As we were on our way for the first set of meetings all our team including myself was attacked with Conjunctivitis, commonly called Pinkeye. Conjunctivitis is caused by a virus that can be dangerous in two ways. First, the person with the infection can lose some of their vision; in severe cases they can totally lose their eyesight. This could be for a short time, or it could be permanent. Second, the infection can spread very rapidly, and is highly infectious. People with "pink eye" often get conjunctivitis germs on their hands by rubbing their eyes, then leave the germs on the objects they touch.

The first sign of this affliction is that your eyes begin to feel dry and irritated. And then it gets to the point where it literally feels like someone has grabbed a handful of sand and shoved it into your eyes, grinding your eyeballs slowly with the sand. The whites of your eyes eventually turn pink, and can become blood red when it's really bad.

The very minute my eyes began to become irritated, I found a quiet place of prayer. I simply spoke to my heavenly Father thanking Him for what **JESUS** had done for me when He had received the stripes upon his back. After meditating upon these realities for a while, it was time to take my authority that **CHRIST** has given to all **Believers**.

I spoke the name of **JESUS** to this affliction, commanding it to go, now, now, now in the name of **JESUS CHRIST** of Nazareth. No ifs, ands or buts! And then I followed through with thanksgiving, praising and thanking **GOD** that I was healed. Not that I was going to be healed, but that I was healed, now! From that moment forward it did not matter how I felt or looked. I knew that I knew that I knew that I was healed. I just kept thanking **GOD** and praising **GOD** quietly, and in my heart.

I went on my way rejoicing even though it did not feel any different, or look any different. Not one more word came out of my mouth to anyone about this affliction, or how terrible my eyes felt. Within less than two days all of the symptoms were gone.

I'm sorry to say that this was not the case for the rest of the team. A lot of these precious people were going through terrible irritation. The brother I had brought with me began to get much worse. Eventually the white of his eyes turned blood red. I knew in my heart that if we did not do something he could go blind.

This continued for over a week, when he finally came to me telling me that he had to get back to America. I have learned a long time ago to not be critical of people, but to work with them where they are at. He told me that I could continue the meetings, but he was leaving. I informed them that I would go with him making sure he was going to get back home. He was my responsibility as his pastor and the **Spirit**ual authority of these meetings.

Of course, my precious Filipino brothers were slightly upset because there were meetings that still needed to be fulfilled. I informed them that I was sorry, but my first responsibility was to this brother, and that the **Holy Ghost** would move through them, and speak through them.

In order to cut our trip short, it was going to take **Faith** to get on the plane earlier than when we were scheduled to leave. And we also had to **Believe** that we were not going to be stopped by customs because of the highly contagious affliction in his eyes. All the way home he kept dark sunglasses on. Through a series of miracles, we were able to board a plane early and get back to America.

The infection that he had picked up in the Philippines did not leave him without medical help. Thank **GOD** he did not lose his eyes. **JESUS** always worked with us where we are at. My position is one of being there for people no matter what. We help, pray and encourage where we can.

If we do not see a miracle we simply keep our eyes on **JESUS**. If we fall short, we just determine in our heart to get back up and keep on going. If I run into situations where it does not seem like I can receive healing, I just go deeper into **GOD**, his word, and his will for my life. *GOD will never let you down!*

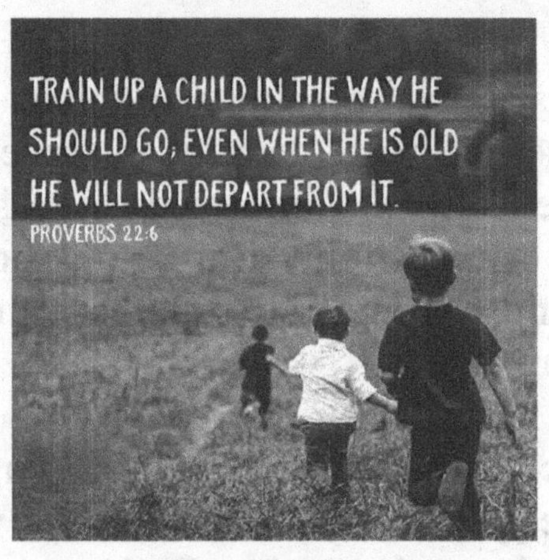

Biblical Training for Children

When I gave my heart to **Christ**, I entered a brand-new world that I never knew existed. As I read my Bible, I immediately recognized that I had to change much of my thinking and belief system. One of these areas was how to raise children.

When I first went to school my parents sent me to a Catholic parochial school, but by the time I hit third grade, they could no longer afford to give me private education. This is when I stepped into a nightmare of the public education school system. I had a number of disadvantages. First, I had a speech impediment that was so bad you could barely understand what I was saying. For years my sister Debbie, who was two years older than me would have to tell people what I said.

The second major issue I had was with my hearing. I was born with immovable bones in my ears, therefore every time I got congested, tremendous pain would hit my head from the pressure. Because I could not hear very well, and people did not clearly understand what I was saying, I was labeled as being mentally retarded. I went through terrible humiliation in the public school to the point where I quit when I was 15 years old.

When I was born again I discovered that the Jewish boys stayed at their daddy side to learn their father's trade. Today we just go off to work and send our children somewhere else to educate them. I decided right then and there that if I was ever going to have any children, they would be at my side. That's how it was carried on through the generations of Abraham all the way up to the times of **Christ**.

Peter the apostle was a fisherman because his daddy was a fisherman. His daddy before him was a fisherman. This passed on from generation to generation. When I discovered this in the Bible I said within my heart, I will teach my boys what I do, for they can do it too. From the time they were little, my three sons and at times my daughter was at my side. If you go into our church, you

**

will see six stone-built fireplaces. I taught my boys to lay those rocks. Most of the work done when it comes to the fireplaces in the church is from my sons.

I also introduced my boys to computer technology, radio station broadcasting, TV broadcasting, and TV editing. My four children have all either written books or are in the midst of writing books.

I've had all my family since they were little out on the streets preaching and sharing the gospel with me. I used to take them into the rough-and-tumble parts of Baltimore and Philadelphia. They have preached the gospel and help feed the hungry for as long as they can remember. They are all preachers of the gospel. I did not force this upon them, I just simply had them at my side with their mother.

Proverbs 22:6 Train up a child in the way he should go, [a]And when he is old he will not depart from it.

1993

The Clinton White House Blues

I should've known better, but stupid is as stupid does they say. Bill Clinton won the election to be the president of the United States. **January 20, 1993 – January 20,**

2001

Immediately immoral and radical stuff began to happen in the White House and in our government. I heard about some of the things that the Clintons were doing, and had done. The next thing I knew I was pulled into all of the scandals of the Clintons. I began to listen to people talking about the Clintons. I even got a videotape of these allegations. Throughout the day I would read the Drudge Report. I would listen to Rush Limbaugh periodically.

"Clinton administration controversies"

0–9
1995 CIA disinformation controversy
1996 United States campaign finance controversy
A
Al-Shifa pharmaceutical factory
Arkansas Project
B
Bill Clinton haircut controversy
Bill Clinton judicial appointment controversies
Almon Glenn Braswell
Juanita Broaddrick
C
Campbell v. Clinton
Hillary Clinton cattle futures controversy
Barrett Report
Henry Cisneros payments controversy
The Clinton Chronicles
Clinton crazies
Clinton health care plan of 1993

Bill Clinton pardon controversy
Clinton v. Jones
Clinton–Lewinsky scandal
Bill Clinton sexual assault and misconduct allegations
Commerce Department trade mission controversy
D
Defense of Marriage Act
Don't ask, don't tell
E
Jeffrey Epstein
F
Gennifer Flowers
Vince Foster
G
Gala Hollywood Farewell Salute to President Clinton
Pincus Green
H
Hollywood fundraiser controversy
I
Impeachment of Bill Clinton
1998 bombing of Iraq
L
Legitimacy of the NATO bombing of Yugoslavia
Lincoln Bedroom for contributors controversy
N
Nannygate
O
Operation Infinite Reach
P
Paul v. Clinton
Political scandals during the Clinton Administration
S
Starr report

T
Timeline of the Cox Report controversy
W
Waco siege
Wampumgate
White House FBI files controversy
White House travel office controversy
Whitewater controversy

Every one of these scandals could have a book written on them, and all of the illegal things that the Clintons committed. Now this is not even including all that Hillary has done up to the present.

You asked me: did it help you at all to know about all this stuff? **Absolutely not**. Plus, it didn't make any difference, and I did not make any difference with this knowledge. You see how the enemy can get us to go on an never ending rabbit trail. It keeps us out of the reality, and the importance of fulfilling **God's** divine plan for our lives. It took me into times of deep despair. We need to keep our eyes on **Jesus Christ** and not the affairs of this world.

LET'S JUMP FORWARD 28 YEARS

Right after my 43rd wedding anniversary, my whole family was hit with Covid. This took place in the year 2021. My seven family members seem to recover relatively quickly. It was a completely different story for me. During that time, I was going through terrible symptoms.

Whenever the enemy attacks me, I immediately get before God to make sure my heart is right. As I cried out to God to speak to me, he brought great repentance into my heart. He began to reveal to me how even though he moved upon my life through the years, yet I had tied his hands. I had unknowingly opened the door to the devil.

A Pandora's box had been swung open. As he took me through the last 28 years, I saw many times where I had missed the will of God. I have already spoken about some of this, especially in my book: I Need God Because I Am Stupid! Yet this visitation from the Lord was even more penetrating. I asked Lord, how did I do this? And he took me back to 1993 when someone gave me VHS tapes about the Clintons. I read about their evil and wicked ways. Even the murdering of witnesses and anyone who got in their way. That list has only grown longer since that time.

The Lord told me that this is the door by which the enemy came sneaking through into not just my life, but my family, in the church I pastor. Up to 1993 my wife and I had simply gone after God. We had tried to keep our eyes upon Jesus Christ. We did not have any form of entertainment, TV, news or even sports. We simply were loving on Jesus, and preaching the gospel of Jesus Christ. But everything changed at that time. We began to get caught up in what was going on politically and nationally. The next thing I knew I was pulled back into watching sports. From there, it became entertainment from Walt Disney and Hollywood.

From there, I progressed into other useless activities like building an ultra glide airplane. Snowmobiling to the point where I had to go up to Ontario to find snow. Building facilities and houses that were not necessary. The list can go on and on of the stupid things that I did even while seeking God. I began to make many wrong decisions when it came to the leadership of the church. Yet despite all of this, God still did amazing miracles, signs, and wonders, and answered prayers. Yet I had opened the door, Pandora's box, by simply watching one set of videotapes about a wicked man and his wife.

Now, as I look at the modern-day church, I see that I am not the only one who har made this mistake. Much of the Pentecostal church, what we call the spirit filled church is completely swallowed up by the wickedness of those in political positions in our nation. Completely swallowed up by the negative news and the evils of the pharmaceutical companies.

When God revealed this to me and opened my eyes, I repented with all of my heart. I believe I have experienced true repentance that is an ongoing process. I am experiencing visitations of the Lord stronger and stronger every day as I focus on my Lord and Savior, Jesus Christ. I hope my sharing of my downfalls will help you to escape the deceptions that have come upon the body of Christ. Jesus did warn us. The Scriptures tell us that the deception will be so great that even those who are lovers of Jesus would almost be deceived.

Dr. Michael H Yeager.

Precise Prophetic Word
to a Rodeo Clown

In one service, there was a married couple who had come forward for prayer. The husband and wife were both working for a youth and children's camp ministry. He was a rodeo clown for the children's camp.

As I came to this couple, the **Spirit** of **GOD** quickened me, and I told them that in three days he would lose his job and position with that ministry. I also told them prophetically that at the time it would seem to be devastating, but that he should not despair, because **GOD** would open up new doors of opportunity for him and his family.

Just as I prophesied, within three days he lost his job—he was fired! Yes, it was extremely devastating for them, but because the Lord had already told him that he was going to have a bright future and a new occupation, they were able to endure this trial. **GOD** supernaturally gave this man favor and he opened up another business that became prosperous.

Prophesied Salvation for her family

One of the mothers in the church came to the front for prayer. The **Spirit** of the Lord quickened me and I prophesied that all of her children would be saved. I also said and that her husband would also be saved, but it would be as if he was snatched from the flames of hell. A number of years later, she related to me that everything I said came to pass. Her husband ended up with cancer. He was not open to the things of **GOD**, but as he lay on the bed of death, he cried out to **JESUS**. He was gloriously saved, with a deep hunger for the things of **GOD**. Shortly thereafter, he slipped off into eternity. He had been snatched from the flames of hell. Here is her story in her own words.

Mary's Testimony:

My name is Mary J. Rockwell. I would like to share three quick testimonies in which I saw **GOD** move in powerful ways in connection to Pastor Mike's prophecy:

Testimony 1: When my children were still in school, I went up to the altar for prayer. Pastor Mike prayed and said, "Your prayers have reached the very throne room of heaven. **GOD** said, " you will live to see all of your children serve the Lord. Your husband will be saved but he will be literally pulled out of the pit at the very end."

My husband, at age seventy-two, contracted cancer from exposure to deadly chemicals while serving in the Marines in Vietnam. I had assumed that he knew the Lord. I prayed for him and said, "I could lay hands on you until you are bald, but you need to cry out to **JESUS** for yourself." He could not say the name, **JESUS** so I knew instantly that it was a demonic block.

I called a local pastor and was about to relate that to

him when he told me that my husband's perception of salvation was wrong and he didn't **Believe** he was really saved. He went to the hospital and prayed with him. My husband called me on the phone and said he had just received **JESUS CHRIST** as his Lord and Savior. His one regret was that he hadn't done enough for the Lord. The Lord had spoken to two young ladies who lived miles away from us to come and pray with him. When they came, my husband prayed for them and they wept and wept.

Three people who were there when Pastor Mike prayed for me called me on the phone and each of them reminded me of the prayer that Pastor Mike had prayed over me many years prior to that. Each of them inquired if my husband was saved and I told them it was just as Pastor Mike had prayed many years before. Since then, two of my four children are serving the Lord...two more to go!

Then Samuel took a vial of oil, and poured it upon his head, and kissed him, and said, is it not because the LORD hath anointed thee to be captain over his inheritance? When thou art departed from me today, then thou shalt Þnd two men by Rachel's sepulchre in the border of Benjamin at Zelzah; and they will say unto thee, The asses which thou wentest to seek are found: and, lo, thy father hath left the care of the asses, and sorroweth for you, saying, What shall I do for my son? (1 Samuel 10:1-2).

Mother Who Was in a Coma

Testimony 2: Years ago my mother was very sick and in the hospital in New York state. I had asked Pastor Mike to pray for me prior to leaving Maryland to go see her. He told me when I saw her I was to pray over her and say, "I command all tormenting mental **Spirit**s to leave her now in **JESUS'** name."

When I arrived at the hospital three of her doctors told me that she was going to die. My sister had called a pastor and began planning for her funeral. She had not eaten for days and had huge bags of fluid in the whites of her eyes and all over her face and didn't even look human. She was hooked up to IVs and monitors. I waited until only she and I were left in the room.

I pulled the curtain around us, put my hands on her head and prayed just as the Lord told me to. I clapped my hands when I said, "Now," and I felt a surge leave my hands and go into her body. The next morning, I went in to see her. The IVs had been removed, she was eating, and all the pockets of fluid had disappeared from her face and eyes! The doctors were amazed. They released her that morning. She lived another three or four years.

Sister in CHRIST Instantly
Had Wrist Healed

Testimony 3: I had fallen and broken both my wrists. The doctor had put a cast on one, but I wouldn't let him cast the other. I went to Pastor Mike's home, and he met me in the driveway. I asked him to pray for my healing, so he did. I went home and within a week I felt that my wrists were healed. I told the doctor either he removes the cast, or I would have my husband cut it off. The doctor had told me I would have to keep it on for several weeks, but he reluctantly removed it. That same week I painted three ceilings by hand. The Lord had totally healed my wrists!

Dad Hagins warning about the Prosperity Gospel!

1. Financial prosperity is not a sign of **God's** blessing. Hagin wrote: "If wealth alone were a sign of **Spirit**uality, then drug traffickers and crime bosses would be **Spirit**ual giants. Material wealth can be connected to the blessings of **God** or it can be totally disconnected from the blessings of **God**."

2. People should never give in order to get. Hagin was critical of those who "try to make the offering plate some kind of heavenly vending machine." He denounced those who link giving to getting, especially those who give cars to get new cars or who give suits to get new suits. He wrote: "There is no **Spirit**ual formula to sow a Ford and reap a Mercedes."

3. It is not biblical to "name your seed" in an offering. Hagin was horrified by this practice, which was popularized in **Faith** conferences during the 1980s. **Faith** preachers sometimes tell donors that when they give in an offering they should claim a specific benefit to get a blessing in return. Hagin rejected this idea and said that focusing on what you are going to receive "corrupts

the very attitude of our giving nature."

4. The "hundredfold return" is not a biblical concept. Hagin did the math and figured out that if this bizarre notion were true, "we would have **Christian**s walking around with not billions or trillions of dollars, but quadrillions of dollars!" He rejected the popular teaching that a **Believer** should claim a specific monetary payback rate.

5. Preachers who claim to have a "debt-breaking" anointing should not be **Trust**ed. Hagin was perplexed by ministers who promise "supernatural debt cancellation" to those who give in certain offerings. He wrote in The Midas Touch: "There is not one bit of Scripture I know about that validates such a practice. I'm afraid it is simply a scheme to raise money for the preacher, and ultimately it can turn out to be dangerous and destructive for all involved.".

CHAPTER FIVE

A Very Important Question!

Does **God** love those who are in hell? Now, why would I ask such a question?

Hopefully you will stop and think. Here is my answer. Who cares!

It does not matter that **God** loves those in hell, even though scripturally I might challenge this theology. It does not make any difference to those who are in hell now. They will never escape from their damnation. They will never have relief from their suffering and pain. They are in hell because they deserve it, because **God** is a just judge. So the fact that **God** loves them does not matter!

Let's bring it to this present generation that is still alive. What does it matter that **God** loves you if you do not respond to his love. In order for **God's** love to save us, we must repent and **Trust** him to have victory over the sin and rebellion in our lives.

We must exercise **Faith** in what **God** has proclaimed is the truth. We must become obsessed, possessed, and consumed with our love and devotion for **Jesus**. Colossians declares--- when **Christ** who is our life shall appear, we shall appear with him in glory.

Here is the very sad truth, many of us ministers today do not love people enough, or even at all, or we would warn them with tears rolling down our faces.

Paul said to the church---------- I ceased not to warn you with tears for three years. May our hearts be broken for the lost and deceived souls that are living self-consumed lives

*Vicky Instantly Delivered from Alcohol

I would rather have this precious sister tell her story, but because she is not here, I'll try my best to tell as much as I know about what happened to this sister in **CHRIST** in this particular service.

The summer of 1993 I was conducting a regular church service at our church in Gettysburg Pennsylvania. I noticed that we had a good handful of visitors that morning, including one particular lady who stood out above the rest because she was rather tall with dark hair. She looked like she was in her early to mid-30s. As I was preaching the word of **GOD**, I could see that the **Spirit** of **GOD** was coming on her in a wonderful way, plus others.

After the message, I gave an altar call for those who needed to get right with **GOD** or needed a **Holy Ghost** touch. I still remember to this day, this particular lady coming forward for **Prayer**. Before I even got a chance to **Pray** for her, she began to shake under the power of the **Holy Ghost**. Something dramatic was happening to her by the **Spirit** of **GOD**. I finally stood in front of her, laying my hands on her gently in the name of **JESUS CHRIST** of Nazareth.

I never, ever put pressure on people's heads when I **Pray** for them. Some ministers I have watched put so much pressure on people's heads to where they're pushing them backward. There are also ministers that I know who use their **Faith** to get people to fall, thinking this is what they need, and it is a sign of **God's** presence. I never do this because it's not the position of the body that matters to me, but what **GOD** is doing in their heart. I have seen people supernaturally touched in a powerful way, walking away transformed without ever falling under the power of **GOD**.

Now in this situation, I barely touched this sisters head when she just crumpled to the floor. She laid on the floor under the power of the **Holy Ghost**, shaking and quivering from head to toe. I moved on to the next person, never realizing what happened that day until about fifteen years later. This precious sister became a member of our church, with her sister and other members of the family.

About fifteen years later, my family and I were over at her family's house celebrating Thanksgiving together. As I was speaking to her about her life, she informed me what happened that day. Someone had invited her to our church service, and she came under the gentle urging of the **Spirit**. Unbeknownst to me, she was an alcoholic. She informed me that even when she came that Sunday morning, she had already been drinking.

She was standing there in our church service drunk under the influence of alcohol. As I was preaching, the **Spirit** of **GOD** began to move on her wonderfully. When I gave the altar call, she could not help but come to the front to be **Prayed** for. The power of the **Holy Ghost** came on her in a mighty way. She found herself lying on the floor. Right then and there, the **Holy Ghost** completely delivered her from alcoholism.

She informed me on that Thanksgiving Day fifteen years later that she never drank another drop from that moment. Thank **GOD** for the **Holy Ghost**, and the wonderful delivering power of the name of **JESUS**. The unclean **Spirit** of the desire of alcohol had come out of her the minute hands were laid upon her

LEARN TO LIVE IN THE QUICKENING!

(To those who have ears to hear)

There is a constant quickening in my heart as I study, meditate, pray, speak, sing the word of **GOD** from my heart. A vibrating, shaking, a deep inner excitement, a fire burning. There is a place where **GOD** can transform you, from glory to glory, even by his **Spirit**!

*Let us go into the DEEP WATERS of THE **SPIRIT**!

This is a place of trembling, walking softly, speaking softly, being ever so sensitive to what the **Spirit** of **GOD** is saying. It is holy ground where not many walk. Come and walk with me into this realm. This is not a place for commonality, self-centeredness, lukewarm passivity.

1 Corinthians 13:11 When I was a child, I spake as a child, I understood as a child, I thought as a child: but when I became a man, I put away childish things.

*Two of the most amazing aspects of who **GOD** is is manifested around us every day of our life!

#1 His Unlimited Power

Hebrews 1:3 Who being the brightness of his glory, and the express image of his person, and upholding all things by the Word Of His Power,, when he had by himself purged our sins, sat down on the right hand of the Majesty on high:

#2 God's **Unlimited Authority**

Ecclesiastes 8:4 Where the word of a king is, there

is power:

What is the one thing that the devil, angels, men want from **GOD** more than anything? This is the one thing from **GOD** that devils, angels, and men still desire?

They want His ABSOLUTE POWER, and His ABSOLUTE AUTHORITY!

A PLACE OF ABSOLUTE POWER, and ABSOLUTE AUTHORITY
(learn to live In the Quickening)

*What the devil and his angels connive, lied, stole, and murdered for has been given freely to **God's** people.

The early church disciples walked and moved, lived and functioned in the power and the authority of **GOD**.

Acts 4:33 And with great power gave the apostles witness of the resurrection of the Lord JESUS: and great grace was upon them all.

Acts 4:30 By stretching forth thine hand to heal; and that signs and wonders may be done by the name of thy holy child JESUS.31 And when they had prayed, the place was shaken where they were assembled together; and they were all filled with the Holy Ghost, and they spake the word of GOD with boldness.

Acts 5:12 And by the hands of the apostles were many signs and wonders wrought among the people;

(and they were all with one accord in Solomon's porch.

Acts 6:8 And Stephen, full of Faith and power, did great wonders and miracles among the people.

1 Thessalonians 1:5 For our gospel came not unto you in word only, but also in power, and in the Holy Ghost, and in much assurance; as ye know what manner of men we were among you for your sake.

Romans 15:19 Through mighty signs and wonders, by the power of the Spirit of GOD; so that from Jerusalem, and round about unto Illyricum, I have fully preached the gospel of CHRIST.

2 Corinthians 12:12 Truly the signs of an apostle were wrought among you in all patience, in signs, and wonders, and mighty deeds.

GODS AUTHORITY AND POWER IS OURS!

Acts 1:8 But ye shall receive power, after that the **Holy Ghost** is come upon you: and ye shall be witnesses unto me both in Jerusalem, and in all Judaea, and in Samaria, and unto the uttermost part of the earth.

Many **Christians** without divine revelation would immediately say: that anybody who was born again, baptized in the **Holy Ghost** can operate in this realm of Amazing Authority and Power! But they would be sadly mistaken. It is given as evidence to this truth by the fact that they are not operating in this Authority and Power.

The proof in the pudding is in the eating.

The demonic world is doing everything they can to keep us out of this realm of **God's** divine authority and power where all things are possible!

How GOD Healed Me of Hernia

***I Kept Radically SHOVING my intestines back into where they belonged with my fingers.**

Day after day we were putting up the steel for our new church facility. We only had the use of the crane for one day. The crane had handled all of the heaviest beams. All of the rest of the steel had to be carried up to the top of the building and placed by hand. I'm not a very large man, as I only weighed about 140 pounds at the time. I was pulling and tugging, walking on steel beams, and balancing precariously with large steel purlins over my shoulder over 20 feet above the ground.

One day, as I was trying to put a heavy beam into place, I felt something rip in my lower abdomen. Later that day I noticed I had a small bulge in my abdomen area. I had torn loose some stomach muscles. I had a hernia! I did not tell anyone. I found a quiet place and cried out to **GOD**. I laid my hands over the hernia, commanding it to go in the name of **JESUS CHRIST** of Nazareth, and I went back to work because the building had to be put up.

Every day I kept on lifting heavy steel. The hernia did not go away so I kept looking to **GOD**, **Trusting**, and believing. The only one who became aware of the hernia was my wife. Honestly, I do not even remember telling her.

Why would I not tell anyone? It wasn't because I was afraid that they would have a poor opinion of me because I wasn't getting healed. I've never worried in the least about people thinking I did not have **Faith**. **Faith** is the substance that is or is not. The Bible says if any man has **Faith**, let him have it to himself.

Romans 14:22 Hast thou Faith? Have it to thyself before GOD.

In my heart, there was nothing I needed to prove to anyone, but to **GOD** himself. You see, my confidence is in **JESUS CHRIST,** the heavenly Father, and the **Holy Ghost**, and the Word of **GOD**! If I have to go to the doctor, or use medication, it's nobody's business.

For over two years this hernia remained with me. Actually, I thought it was three, but my wife says it was two. Every time this hernia would bother me, I would lay hands over the top of it, and command it to go, thanking **GOD** that I was healed.

Eventually, this hernia began to get very serious. It began to bulge so far from my body that I knew eventually it would strangle. A strangled hernia is very dangerous.

A strangulated hernia is a hernia that is cutting off the blood supply to the intestines and tissues in the abdomen. Symptoms of a strangulated hernia include pain near a hernia that gets worse very quickly and may be associated with other symptoms.

I knew in my heart that it was time to get very serious about this situation. You see the kingdom of heaven sufferings violence and the violent take it by force. I knew that I knew that I knew that by the stripes of **JESUS** I am healed. I literally began to take the fingers of my right hand shoving this hernia back up into my stomach lining, and speaking to my stomach lining and commanding it to be healed. For approximately two weeks I kept on aggressively shoving this hernia back into my body, declaring that it was healed.

In the world they say: it's the early bird that gets the worm. In **Christianity**: It's the **Spirit**ually Violent Man That Gets the Answer.

Now, this type of **Faith** needs to be developed. It's absolute unwavering, and total confidence, I cannot be defeated attitude and **GOD**.

Hebrews 6:18that by two immutable things, in which it was impossible for GOD to lie, we might have a strong consolation, who have fled for refuge to lay hold upon the hope set before us:

I went to bed one night approximately two weeks after I had become aggressive with my **Faith** in **CHRIST and** woke up the next morning to an amazing miracle. The hernia was completely gone. That has been over 30 years ago, and it has never come back. **Faith** is the substance of things hoped for, the evidence of things not seen!

No more vaccinations

It was time to take my two sons in for boosters of their vaccinations. As we sat in the clinic waiting, I picked up a flyer that you could read about vaccinations. As I read their literature, I could hardly **Believe** my eyes. It was giving the stats of what happens to some who receive these shots.

I thought back when I had Michael as a baby receive his shots. He became extremely sick and congested. I walked the floor for hours and days praying over him and binding the sickness. The congestion was so bad that he could barely breathe at times. Now, as I looked back I realize that Michael got extremely sick after he received those shots. Daniel also went through the same situation!

The polio vaccines heralded the elimination of polio from the U.S., saving countless children from sudden paralysis and death. In the developing world, however, outbreaks of poliovirus still occur sporadically, an ironic consequence of the polio vaccine itself. A new genetic study of the vaccine poliovirus reveals how this happens in real time. About 1 of every 1,000 cases will cause paralysis.

After I read this flyer, I whispered to my boys, come on boys let's go! I quietly got up and walked out with my sons from that clinic. We never went back. My son Steven and Daughter Stephanie have never received vaccinates, and they also have seldom ever been sick. My Daughter has never needed medical help!

Daniels face covered with sugar

My son Daniel was absolutely addicted to sugar when he was about six years old. We had to hide everything sweet from him. One morning I heard some noise coming from our kitchen. I tiptoed down to the kitchen to see what was going on.

As I peeked around the corner I saw Daniel up on the counter top. He had a bag of white sugar in his little hands. His face and little hands were covered in sugar. Plus the counter top was also coated in white sugar like it was snowing.

Of course I ran over to him and took away the sugar bag. I had to basically give him a bath. For many years after that we kept all sugar and sweets out of the house.

Family Camping but Where Is Dad?

As I look back across my life there are times that I am filled with great regrets. Now, I know a lot of the present theology in the pulpit is that we should have no regrets. But this teaching, reminds me of the truth that a famous historian spoke: **He That Forgets**

History, Is Doomed to Repeat It.

We need to live and learn from all the mistakes that we have made through the years if we are going to have any improvements. It is called **The School of Hard Knocks**. Yes I am filled with regrets, and yet there is no condemnation because I know I am forgiven. Yet even though I'm forgiven it does not change the fact of what happened.

I thank **God** that my wife was the one who wanted to spend time with the children camping. I would reluctantly agree with her, yet I was so busy that I thought it would be more important for me to be at the church, busy about ministry. But every year she was **Faith**ful to get everything ready to go camping. We had an old pop-up camper that basically was run down. She sewed all the canvas with different colours of material wherever there were rips. The crank did not work, so we had to lift it in place manually from the inside. Then we would prop up for precisely cut two by fours in each corner.

Kathy and the kids would pack the camper with all that we would need for a three day to five-day camp out. There is a beautiful park right across the mountain from us called Caledonia State Park. This is where we would set up the camp. I would pull the camper with my truck to the campsite. Then I would set everything up in a hurry because I needed to get back to the office.

After I did everything that they needed help to do, I'd hop in my truck and off to work I go. At the end of the busy workday in the office I would head back to the campsite. We would have a campfire, laugh a little and have some fun, then get the kids into their sleeping bags. And to bed we would go. In the morning I was made to breakfast, but as soon as breakfast was over with, I'd head back to the office. I had ants in my pants, and I could not stay at the campsite with my family because I thought what I was doing was so important.

Tubes Tied While Still Alive

My wife gave birth to our fourth child, **Stephanie joy Yeager**. She had a difficult time during this pregnancy. The weight that it put upon her stomach muscles and her back became so traumatic that she decided not to have any more children. **I wanted a dozen!**

She informed me that she was going to have her tubes tied. I was against this because I have heard negative information about this procedure and what women go through when they have their tubes tied.

What are the risks of a tubal ligation?
1, Bleeding from an incision or inside the abdomen.
2, Infection.
3, Damage to other organs inside the abdomen.
4, Side effects from anesthesia.
5, Ectopic pregnancy (an egg that becomes fertilized outside the uterus)
6, Incomplete closing of a fallopian tube that results in pregnancy.
7, It is Permanent.
8, Many women gain weight after the procedure.

I was wholeheartedly against her receiving this procedure. I told her that if I needed to I would get a vasectomy so she would not have to be afraid of getting pregnant. I did not want her to go through the negative results that could come because of having her tubes tied. At that time though I did not realize the negative effects that a vasectomy would have on me, let alone the procedure I went through.

A vasectomy is a common surgical procedure whereby the vas deferens – the tubes that carry sperm to the semen – are cut and tied to prevent fertility. It's especially common in older men who have already had children, but there's an increasing movement of younger men undergoing the procedure after making a decision that they don't want to have kids and don't want to take any risks when it comes to what contraception they and their partners are using.

There are plenty of things that people don't tell you about a vasectomy before you (or your partner) are about to undergo one.

It is Linked with Prostate Cancer.

Something that may be a deterrent for some people is the fact that the procedure has been linked with prostate cancer. In a study by the Health professionals at Harvard School of Public Health, it was found that those who had had the procedure were 150% more likely to develop the condition later in life. This study used a sample of 50,000 men.

We got a hold of the doctor who delivered our first son Michael, which also delivered my wife, and delivered her mother. Three generations so you know he was extremely old. When we had a consultation he knew that I was a pastor so he would give me a special deal. $50 is what he told me that he could do the operation for. **I found out the hard way that you get what you pay for.**

So I went to his office McConnellsburg Pennsylvania. He took me into their sterilized room with his helper. Then he laid me on the couch and gave me a localized shot to kill the pain. He told me this would not take very long and so I waited for him to begin the procedure.

Well, he had his scalpel and his equipment are set aside. He went to make the incision, but I was still alive. Pain shot through my body as he began to cut. I told him that I could still feel everything he was doing. He said OKAY I'll give you another local shot. About 10 minutes later he came back to try again, but I was still alive. I **Believe** this happened three times, and I could still feel everything.

He finally said he needed to get this job done so he rolled up a washcloth and told me to open my mouth. He stuck it in my mouth and told me to clamp down. I should've got up off the table right then and there. This time he just kept cutting away as I was clamping down on the washcloth as hard as I could with my teeth. And then he sewed me back up with me still being alive.

My wife took me home, and I went through a period of tremendous pain and soreness. One day as I was examining the job he had done I saw like a small miniature tube sticking out from my private. I could hardly **Believe** what I was seeing. Him being in his late 80s he must not have been able to see very well, because my tube was sticking out in the open air. Eventually it dried up and fell off.

A number of years later I began to experience tremendous pain. It felt like somebody had kicked me very hard between my legs. As I went on the Internet and began to investigate, I discovered that this is one of the side effects of having a vasectomy. Through the years I have had to stand against this pain, even at this present moment as I write this book I'm having to deal with this pain. If I had to do it all over again, I definitely would not have had it done. We could have found some other way in order to prevent my wife from getting pregnant again. As the saying goes: **Stupid Is As Stupid Does!**

Bouncing My Plane at 5000 feet

My Amazing Journey - Doc Yeager

As a student pilot I had to register a certain amount of mileage of flying by myself. This was daytime and nighttime flight. They scheduled me to fly up to the Poconos giving me specific instructions of what airport to land at. It was going be a three-tier flight. That means I was going to be visiting three airports before my final destination home.

At ground level it was pretty calm, but as I began to reach the altitude in which I was required to fly the weather began to get rather rough. As I was going over the mountains of the Poconos of fierce wind took a hold of me. Now, I did not have my seatbelt on at this time, so when I hit this turbulent wind it began to bounce my plane in almost the same way somebody would bounce a basketball.

My wings on my little Cessna 150 were going up and down like a bird flapping its wings. I was wondering how much abuse this little plane could put up with. My Cessna 150 was rising and falling so fast that my head was literally hitting the ceiling of the cockpit. I quickly tightened my seatbelt for that my head would not hit the ceiling of the cockpit any longer. I gave the plane full throttle hoping that I could get out of this severe and turbulent wind. Thank **God** eventually my plane began to smooth out.

As I look back over that experience I think it was partly my fault for not checking the exact weather conditions of where I was flying.

IN-FLIGHT ADVISORIES warn pilots of potentially hazardous weather. They include SIGMETs, CONVECTIVE SIGMETs, AIRMETs, and Center Weather Advisories (CWA). ... SIGMETs are issued as needed. AIRMET bulletins are issued routinely and supplement the Area Forecast (FA).

AIRMETs focus on weather that may adversely affect aircraft safety in still-flyable weather. ... SIGMETs, which come in non-convective and convective types, focus on more severe weather conditions.

Landed My Plane in the Wrong Direction

One of my required trips took me all the way down into a major Delaware airport. As I was approaching the airport, I radioed in.

Tower this is "Cessna 92747 requesting permission to land. By the way I am a student pilot." The tower came back with permission for me to land informing me to land from a specific direction. I affirm that I had received my instructions. I could see the runway directly ahead of me. As I lined up to come in for a landing, the tower once again spoke to me. Cessna 92747 you are coming in the wrong way, but that's okay. You just come in the way you're coming; we have cleared the traffic for you.

Of course, I was extremely embarrassed but what can a student pilot do? I wasn't going to argue with them, and I was grateful that they had cleared the traffic for their safety and mine. I did make a pretty good touchdown. Basically, it was going to be a touching and go.

As a student pilot I had to park the airplane, get out and do a walk around. Plus I needed to stretch my limbs because I had been cramped up in that little Cessna for quite a number of hours. Once I was back seated in the plane I received permission to leave.

This time I left the airport on the runway in the right direction. As I look over my experiences in flying I am so grateful for **God's** mercy and help. Many times I could've easily crashed and died.

If You Buy that Airplane You'll Die

I was learning how to fly a single prop plane. I had already finished my ground school and was in possession of my student pilot license. I had just started my cross-country flights. I had been praying and thinking about how I could cover my cost and yet make money flying.

Somebody shared with me that the flying school in Shippensburg was selling their Cessna 172 for a good price. I contacted the owners of this plane. It was in beautiful shape. I went through the process of purchasing it. I went to the airport in York, where I was flying out of, to see if they were interested in renting this plane from me once I purchased it. They said they absolutely were.

By the time everything was said and done, I had the financial backing for this plane, plus the airport was going to rent it from me. So, the end results were a win-win situation. I was going to have my own plane totally taken care of for free! Plus, I was going to be making good money from it. During this time, I was also in need of a pickup truck. I had sold my last truck and given the money to the church. I did not want a new truck, just one that would get me around. My wife informed me that her brother was selling his Ford pickup.

One day as I was in prayer, the **Spirit** of **GOD** spoke to me, and this is what He said: "if you buy this plane your whole family will die in it." The second thing he told me is that if I bought this pickup truck, I would not only lose all the money I invested in buying it, but that it would cost me more than what I invested into it. I knew the voice of **GOD**!

I knew if **GOD** said that we would die in this plane if I bought it, we would die in the plane just as He had said. I did not care how good the deal was or how much money I could make off of it. I called the airport, and the owners of the airplane. I told them that I was not going to buy the plane, and that I was so sorry for any of their wasted time and energy.

If You Buy the F250 you will Lose Your Money

I was confronted with what to do about my brother-in-law's pickup truck. For some reason I just did not want to let go of it. In spite of **GOD** telling me what would happen, I decided to buy it. I called up my brother-in-law and told him my decision to buy his truck. Amazingly, he spent a good amount of time trying to convince me not to buy it. I had made up my mind; I wanted his F-250 three-quarter ton pickup truck.

I bought his truck, and almost immediately the engine went bad, then the transmission went bad. After I had taken care of these two major problems I thought to myself, I better sell it before I lose all of my money. I put it up for sale as is. A young man came by really wanting my truck. I told him he was going to have to buy the truck as it was with no guarantees. He completely agreed. He bought the truck, and drove away with it.

Within three days, he was back on my doorstep mad as a hornet. He said the frame of the truck was bent and he wanted some of his money back. I reminded him that he had bought the truck as is with no guarantees. He said he did not give a flip, the frame was bent, and he should get back some of his money. I ended up giving him back some of his money.

When all was said and done, I lost more money than I had invested. It was the voice of **GOD** telling me not to buy the truck! Thank you, **JESUS**, that I did not buy the Cessna 172. If I would have, you would not be reading this book now!

Now when much time was spent, and when sailing was now dangerous, because the fast was now already past, Paul admonished them, And said unto them, Sirs, I perceive that this voyage will be with hurt and much damage, not only of the lading and ship, but also of our lives. Nevertheless the centurion Believed the master and the owner of the ship, more than those things which were spoken by Paul (Acts 27:9-11).

CHAPTER SIX

Flew my airplane
through a set of high lines.

I was in the midst of receiving my airplane license. I had finished ground school and had completed all of my cross country flying. One day I was at the York airport doing simple go-arounds (That's where you land and you just keep going after you land and take back off again).

I later found out that the Spirit of GOD had quickened my wife and told her to pray for me. She had already been really upset at me for wasting all of this money on flying. The Lord told her that if she did not forgive me and get her heart right, I was going to die. She repented, and cried out to GOD, and said, "Lord, I give it to you. Please protect him."

Everything seemed to be going okay as I did go-arounds, but as I was getting ready to land, the wind shifted to another direction. They called me from the tower and told me that they felt it should still be okay to stay in the same pattern one more Time; and that the next Time around I could land in the opposite direction.

As I made my approach for the runway, I began to meticulously go through all of the processes of making a proper landing. I lowered my flaps, turned on my carburetor deicer, and began to bring my airspeed down to where I would be landing at about forty mph. I was still about 30 feet above the runway. Everything seemed perfectly normal.

As I began to pull back on the yoke to flare the plane, all of a sudden, my speed indicator dropped to zero. As a young pilot, I did not realize what this meant. It was an indication that the wind was now coming in from behind me. This meant I had just lost all of my lift. I dropped like a rock, and my plane slammed into the runway. I hit the runway very hard. I pulled back on the yoke.

The minute I slammed into the runway; I bounced back up into the air like a basketball. I made a terrible mistake: instead of going around, once again, I pulled back on the yoke and tried to land my plane. Once again, I dropped like a rock, slamming just as hard into the runway as the last Time. Not being very intelligent, I tried to land once again. This Time when I bounced I was really in trouble.

Now my plane was wholly turned away from the runway. There was nothing but a grassy field ahead of me with electrical power lines. I gave the little Cessna 152 full power. I kept my flaps down, in take-off position. Yet, I made another major mistake by keeping my carburetor deicer on. This means I did not have the full horsepower of my engine.

Now, I was headed right for the power lines! My airspeed was barely enough to keep me in the air. I knew that I could not turn away from the power lines. Plus, there were trees right before you reach the high lines. If I tried to turn away, I was a dead man.

Moreover, I knew that I didn't have enough skill to fly underneath them by getting between them and the trees. In addition, I knew that I could not get over the top of them. If I pulled back too much on the yoke, it would cause the plane to go higher, but it would drop like a rock again because my airspeed was way too slow. My plane would stall and I would nose dive right into the ground.

At that very moment, I knew I was a dead man. Time itself seemed to stand still. My whole life flashed in front of me in a matter of seconds. My heart was filled with thankfulness to GOD for all the wonderful things He had done for me in my life, for giving me my precious wife and four beautiful children. The second thing that hit me was tremendous sorrow and regret: I would never see my beautiful wife, Kathleen, again in this world—I would never be able to hold her in my arms, never be able to hold my three sons and precious little girl to my chest.

I desperately wanted to get on the radio and tell the tower operators to tell my wife and my children that I was so very sorry and that I loved them beyond expression. I wanted to tell my wife and kids that I wished I could be there to see them graduate from school and one day get married—to see my precious girl walking down the aisle to stand at the side of her groom. But my Time had run out. I did not have Time to say my good-byes. I was headed straight for the power lines.

As I approached my inevitable death, these electrical power lines filled my eyes. It was as if the wires were magnified in size. They looked to be six inches wide in diameter. They filled the windshield of my plane.

I realize that the wires are not anywhere near that size, but as I approached them, that's how I saw them. At that moment, all I could do was cry out for JESUS. The next thing I knew, I was through into the power lines and through them. I went right through them! I did not go underneath them, and I did not go over the top of them. Supernaturally the power lines had to have gone right through my plane.

As I flew my plane straight ahead, I was overwhelmed with amazement, thankfulness, and tremendous joy. I kept rehearsing over and over in my mind what had just happened. Could it really be? Did I go through the power lines? I know I did. I was headed right into the wires. Amazing! The tower kept calling out to me over the radio, "Mike, are you there? Are you okay? Please answer!"

They had, to some extent, seen what happened. When they finally got me to respond, all they could get out of me was, "Thank You JESUS! Thank you, JESUS! Thank you, JESUS!" Three other airports also picked up the airport radio frequency at that Time. All the traffic controllers and radio personnel on that frequency heard me say over and over, "Thank you, JESUS!"

After I landed, the mechanical personnel took the plane into the hangar. They had seen me slamming into the runway. In their thoughts, there is no way that this plane did not have structural damage. They went over it with a fine-toothed comb. Amazingly, they came back with a report that everything was absolutely fine.

(2 Chronicles 7:3).And when all the children of Israel saw how the þre came down, and the glory of the LORD upon the house, they bowed themselves with their faces to the ground upon the pavement, and worshipped, and praised the LORD, saying, For he is good; for his mercy endureth for ever.

Kathleen's perspective:

My husband had disappeared early in the morning. He probably told me where he was going while I was still asleep, but I never remembered. As the day went on, I decided to call his cell phone to figure out where he was. After several futile calls, I called Debra, Mike's sister, who worked in our church office at the Time.

Upon hearing that he had gone for flying lessons, my anger began to rise. My thoughts were, who does he think he is, going off and spending thousands of dollars on flying lessons, when we have enough bills to pay, and we need things for the house, the children, and me!

Immediately, the Spirit of GOD arrested me and rebuked me. Within my Spirit came: which is more important, the money, or your husband's life?

Brokenness clenched my soul, and I quickly repented. Asking GOD to forgive me for my selfishness, I told the Lord that my husband was more important than millions of dollars and that the money wasn't worth Mike's life!

The devil had lost the battle to keep me bitter and unforgiving, and the unity between us, as husband and wife, was not broken. Directly, a Spirit of fear tried to grip my heart, and I knew that fear was another tool of the devil to bring division and destruction. An urgency to pray and to stand in Faith made me stop everything!

To this day, I remember where I was sitting when I began to pray: right at our kitchen bar. As I sat on the barstool reiterating my repentance of selfishness, I implored the Lord to spare Mike's life, keep him safe, and bring him back to the children and me. Little did I know that I was genuinely pleading for my husband's life!

Through my tears, I remember boldly declaring, "Lord, You've given Your angels charge over us, to keep us in all of our ways, even in our stupidity." My declaration continued, "In our pathway is life, and there is no death. So, Father, I put Michael in your hands.

"I know you'll bring him home safely."

At this point, I made a covenant in my heart. I made my stand, "I Trust You, Lord because there is no one else to Trust. If I Can't Trust You to keep Mike safe, then I can Trust no one. Thank You for bringing my husband back to me!" I refused to give in to bitterness, fear, or worry. My hope was in the Lord, who is always Faithful.

The devil had lost the fight on my side to cause division, bitterness, anger, fear, and lack of peace. I did not fail to repent and intercede for my husband when the Spirit of GOD dealt with me. God's grace had helped me through the test. God's Faith had brought victory and brought my husband home alive. When Mike came through the door of our home that day, he told me of his near-fatal flight.

My response was, "If the Lord hadn't dealt with my heart, you might have eaten those power lines!" I embraced Mike with a thankful heart and a grace in my heart towards the Lord's goodness and mercy. GOD surely knew what He was doing in both of our lives to keep us under His protection. If I had given in to bitterness and fear or failed to intercede and stand in Faith, I may not have my husband today!

Be ye angry, and sin not: let not the sun go down upon your wrath: Neither give place to the devil (Ephesians 4:26-27).

Matthew 7:21 Not every one that saith unto me, Lord, Lord, shall enter into the kingdom of heaven; but he that doeth the

will of my Father which is in heaven. 22 Many will say to me in that day, Lord, Lord, have we not prophesied in thy name? and in thy name have cast out devils? and in thy name done many wonderful works? 23 And then will I profess unto them, I never knew you: depart from me, ye that work iniquity. "Forgive, and the Lord will forgive you."

A New Flight Instructor Total Disaster

With what I had just been through in flying my plane through those high-power lines, I was really being shook. When I went back to the York airport to fly once again, my instructor informed me that he was being elevated into a higher position. That he would no longer be able to train me when it came to flying. Here was another situation that was shaking me up. My flight instructor introduced me to the young buck who was going to take his place. Right away the red lights began to go off.

I sat down and spoke for a while with the new instructor and then he said let's go out to the plane. From that moment forward it was a disaster. Nothing I did was right in this man's eyes. He Nick picked every little thing I did which he said in his opinion was wrong. All that the previous instructor had taught me he was telling me was wrong and that I needed to do it his way. As I look back at that moment I was extremely upset, disappointed, discouraged and I didn't know what to do. Yet, **all things work together for good to them that love God that are called according to his purpose. God** was going to take this situation and use it to get me free from the Obsession of having to fly my own plane.

I left the airport that day totally rejected Docd defeated in my heart. Yet I was not ready to give up my obsession with flying. I was experiencing dreams where I saw myself and my whole family in the plane crashing and burning. It was the **Spirit** of **God** trying to warn me of what would happen if I kept on pursuing the direction I was going.

My Last Flight as a pilot 6/1/89

I decided to go for a flight by myself to try to get back some of my confidence. I still remember that day as I crawled into the rented Cessna 150. Checking all the instruments and all the readouts. Pulling back and forth on the yoke. Checking the rudder pedals and brake pedals. Lifting and lowering the flaps.

I taxied out to the runway waiting for permission to fly. I pushed on the brakes and gave it full throttle until my little plane was shaking. Then I released the brake pedals, and down the runway I went. Pushing the yoke in all the way for that the plane would not take off until it had built up enough speed. Once I had reached my prescribed speed, I pulled back very easy on the yoke, as I lifted gently off of the ground.

When I finally attained the proper altitude at about 5000 feet above the ground, I just simply flew. I flew over the countryside breathing in the freedom of being able to fly with no restraints.

I still remember as the sun was setting, I came back in for my final approach and landing. At that moment I had not decided this was my last time, but something within my heart must've told me.

A sadness came upon my heart as I walked away from that plane, and the airport. As I drove home I reflected on what was really important to me. My relationship with **Christ**, my lovely wife, and my children. **God** had been so good even in the midst of extreme danger he had preserved and kept me.

Another Kenneth Copeland or Charles Capps

Dr. Clifford Rice had come to minister in our church. He knew that I had become a student pilot and that I was flying. One morning as we were eating breakfast, he simply looked at me, and said this: **why are you flying?** I told him I wanted to use flying to get me to where I needed to go to preach the gospel.

He then informed me that he used to be a pilot, and that he stopped because it was dangerous. Statistics will try to tell you that you flying a plane is safer than driving a car pertaining to how many miles you travel, but this is not true. He then began to tell me of people that he had personally known who had died in planes.

He told me unless you are flying for business daily you are looking for trouble. You need to develop skills when it comes to flying, and only those who fly for a living really are prepared for situations where most don't know what to do. He said: Mike you have too many irons in the fire. You are way him too distracted. Flying is serious business. Then he told me about a wealthy friend of his who thought he was really good at flying, but he also himself had too many irons in the fire. Eventually it caught up to him and he died in a terrible plane accident.

He said: Michael you're going to get yourself killed and leave your family with no husband or father. He said to me: let me just be blunt, you simply want to be **another Kenneth Copeland or Charles Capps.** The minute he said that conviction overwhelmed me. He had stripped me bear to my bones. In my heart of hearts, I knew what he said was true. I began to weep almost uncontrollably at that moment. I told Dr. Rice and my wife that I was done flying. I was going to hang up my wings and keep my feet on the earth.

That morning at our Sunday service I stood before our congregation, and I confess to them my sin. That I had been flying because I wanted to be **another Kenneth Copeland or Charles Capps.** I closed the door on the devil that morning from snuffing my life out with a plane accident because of the hidden pride that had been in my heart.

Daniel Broke His Arm Because of My Pride

We were camping at Caledonia state park. We also brought bikes for the children. It was in the morning, and we had just finished eating breakfast. Danny went to ride a girl's bike we had brought with us. He had just learned how to ride a bike but was still very wobbly! When I saw him riding the girl's bike, I told him to stop and get off it! He tried to tell me the boy's bike was too big for him. I would not listen though and insisted he get off the girl's bike. Well, I am sorry to say he listened to me.

I went over and helped him get on the boy's bike. I shoved him of as he went down the road very wobbly. About 30 feet from me I watched Daniel in slow motion take a nosedive. I ran as fast as I could to his side. As quickly as I could I got him out from underneath the bike. Immediately I noticed his left arm was bent in a strange way. Here he had broken one of the bones in his arm.

Oh, how my heart broke at that moment. It was all my fault. I'm the one because of pride that said he could not ride the girl's bike. Now, here my son was with the broken arm that was bent like a banana. I rushed him over to the car. Strapping them into the passenger seat and headed off to the hospital.

As I drove into the hospital I little do was to the point of almost weeping. I kept telling him that I was so sorry for what I had done. He just sat there looking up at me not saying a word. He wasn't complaining, or crying, he was simply cradling his broken bent arm with his good arm.

I finally got them into the emergency room, where we sat and waited for the first available Doctor.

You Better Back off Doc

When my son and I were finally ushered into the presence of the doctor, he was a huge man sitting behind the desk. He told my son Daniel to come over to him. He then proceeded to grab his arm in a very rough way and began to twist it. With no compassion or concern about the pain my son was going through he was acting like a bull in a china closet.

Tremendous anger exploded in my heart. Not an anger built upon bitterness or hate but out of love for my son. I jumped towards that Dr. faster than I could think. I put my finger in his ugly face and told him: **get your hands off my son. Don't you ever handle him in that way again**. I mean I was so angry I could have spit bullets.

The Doctors face turned ashen white, and he took his hands off my son. He just stared at me with a surprised look on his face. He did not speak a word. Then he finally said: we will schedule for him to have this arm fixed. Then I took my son Daniel and left his office.

When this procedure was scheduled, my wife came in. She sat with Daniel and waited until he was ushered into the surgery room. The good news is they did not have to perform surgery. They x-rayed his arm and set it back in place with him sedated. For the next two months he had to wear a plaster cast. Thank **God** he fully recovered from my stupidity.

In most cases it takes around 6 to 8 weeks to recover from a broken arm or wrist. It can take longer if your arm or wrist was severely damaged. You will need to wear your plaster cast until the broken bone heals. The skin under the cast may be itchy for a few days but this should pass.

*I should have told the gas station owner

The major mistake I made in this situation is that I believed I had more **Time** to share the gospel with my neighbor. Surely a couple of hours would make no difference. But, oh, was I wrong!

It was the Fourth of July weekend. I had stopped at the local convenience store to pick up some items to take to my wife's family reunion. Every Fourth of July, all her relatives on her mother's side would get together. We were running late, as usual. I was trying to get some things done before we left. As I entered the convenience store, I saw the owner of the property standing behind the counter. I had spoken to him a little bit in the past but never in great depth.

The minute I saw him, the **Spirit** of **God** quickened my heart to speak to him about **JESUS**; the only problem was that I was running extremely late. My wife and children would be upset with me if I did not get home soon. So, I argued with **GOD** and told him that I would stop and speak to him as soon as I got home from my wife's family reunion. Tremendous conviction began to flood my soul, but I ignored it. One would think that I would have learned my lesson from the last devastating experience; the **Time** that I was supposed to talk to Billy but did not. Billy had died shortly afterward in a head-on collision.

I went home and quickly loaded up all of the picnic supplies and food, forgetting all about the convenience store owner. I got my family into the car and we went to

Kathleen's Fourth of July family reunion. Approximately four hours later that day, we returned back home. On the way, I decided to pull into the convenience store. When I pulled into the parking lot, I noticed there was something wrong. They did not have any business which was highly unusual. Not a single vehicle in the parking lot was to be seen.

A very bad feeling came over me. I walked up to the store doors and discovered them locked. To my dismay, there was a notice on the door that said, "CLOSED DUE TO DEATH IN THE FAMILY." That afternoon, the owner of the store had died from a heart attack. I should have shared **JESUS** with him when the Lord had prompted mc to earlier that day. Lord have mercy! The moment **GOD** speaks, we need to obey!

For he saith, I have heard thee in a Time accepted, and in the day of salvation have I succoured thee: behold, now is the accepted Time; behold, now is the day of salvation (2 Corinthians 6:2).

1 Timothy 5:1Rebuke not an elder, but intreat him as a father; and the younger men as brethren;

1 Timothy 5:17Let the elders that rule well be counted worthy of double honour, especially they who labour in the word and doctrine.

1 Timothy 5:19Against an elder receive not an accusation, but before two or three witnesses.

Titus 1:5 For this cause left I thee in Crete, that thou shouldest set in order the things that are wanting, and ordain elders in

every city, as I had appointed thee:6 If any be blameless, the husband of one wife, having Faithful children not accused of riot or unruly.

CHAPTER SEVEN

Laughed at my Tormented Brother

As I write my autobiography, I am sharing with you many things that I am ashamed of. May the Lord have mercy on all of us. So many times, in our life we do not really stop and consider the consequences of our actions. This story is one of the events that if I could do it all over again I would. It completely changed the course of the direction for my younger brother and his family's life.

My brother Dan was six years younger than me. While he was in the Army, I had led him to the Lord. He had also been filled with the **Holy Ghost**. Once he was discharged from the Army, he brought his wife Lisa and their children to live in our community in Pennsylvania. He actually lived in the same house that I had bought. They lived on the second floor.

They finally bought their own small house up on the side of the mountain. When I had built my new house next to the church he would come over and pray in my basement with me. Now, Daniel had always been a tormented soul. I really did not understand what he was going through, until some years later I went through a valley of tremendous torment. It was after our little girl Naomi had been seriously injured, and our church was falling apart, including my marriage. That's a story for another time. Thank the Lord **Jesus** that **God** rescued the church and our marriage.

One day Daniel and I was in my basement praying. I looked over at him, and his face was so twisted and in deep agony that it struck me as being extremely hilarious. I had no idea that what I was about to do would separate my brother and I for the rest of our life's. I just started laughing. I must've said something about the look on his face. At that moment he became extremely offended and stormed out of my basement.

He had been attending our church up to that time, but from that moment forward he never came back. I never apologized because I was blind to what I had done for years after that. In a number of months he moved his whole family out West to be with one of my uncles. Now this uncle was a Jehovah witness and did not **Believe** that **Jesus** was **God** manifested in the flesh.

Because of my stupidity it opened the door for my brother Daniel to take in false doctrines. Eventually he **Believe**d the lie that **Jesus** was not **God** manifested in the flesh. Then he embraced universalism which teaches the false doctrine that there is no hell, there is no judgment for wickedness, and that everybody's going to go to heaven. I have had to stop communicating with him years ago because he was constantly attacking me about what I **Believe**.

***Let this be a warning to all of us and in how we respond and minister to people. Just one stupid thing can destroy the lives of those who are living in a place of torment and sorrow.**

God's Got Your Number

I met Ken Gaub many years ago. He has been to our church numerous times to minister. He wrote a wonderful book called **"God's Got Your Number"**. This book is filled with tremendous testimonies of **God's** divine interventions and answers to prayers. Ken gave me permission to share this story.

From Kens Gaubs own words: I was driving on 1-75 near Dayton, Ohio, with my wife and children in our coach bus. We turned off the highway for a rest and refreshment stop. My wife Barbara and children went into the restaurant. I suddenly felt the need to stretch my legs, so waved them off ahead saying I'd join them later. I bought a soft drink, and as I walked toward a Dairy Queen, feelings of self-pity enshrouded my mind. I loved the Lord and my ministry, but I felt drained, burdened. My cup was empty.

Suddenly the impatient ringing of a telephone nearby jarred me out of my doldrums. It was coming from a phone booth at a service station on the corner. Wasn't anyone going to answer the phone? Noise from the traffic flowing through the busy intersection must have drowned out the sound because the service station attendant continued looking after his customers, oblivious to the ringing.

."Why doesn't somebody answer that phone?" I muttered. .I began reasoning. It may be important. What if it's an emergency? Curiosity overcame my indifference. I stepped inside the booth and picked up the phone.

"Hello," I said casually and took a big sip of my drink. The operator said: "Long distance call for Ken Gaub. "My eyes widened, and I almost choked on a chunk of ice. Swallowing hard, I said, "You're crazy!" Then realizing I shouldn't speak to an operator like that, I added, "This can't be! I was walking down the road, not bothering anyone, and the phone was ringing... "Is Ken Gaub there?" the operator interrupted, "I have a long distance call for him. "It took a moment to gain control of my babbling, but I finally replied, "Yes, he is here. "Searching for a possible explanation, I wondered if I could possibly be on Candid Camera!

Still shaken, perplexed, I asked, "How in the world did you reach me here? I was walking down the road, the pay phone started ringing, and I just answered it on chance. You can't mean me.". "Well," the operator asked, "Is Mr. Gaub there, or isn't he?" "Yes, I am Ken Gaub," I said, finally convinced by the tone of her voice that the call was real. Then I heard another voice say, "Yes, that's him, operator. That's Ken Gaub. I listened dumbfounded to a strange voice identify herself. "I'm Millie from Harrisburg, Pennsylvania. You don't know me, Mr. Gaub, but I'm desperate. Please help me." "What can I do for you?".

She began weeping. Finally she regained control and continued. "I was about to commit suicide, had just finished writing a note, when I began to pray and tell **GOD** I really didn't want to do this. Then I suddenly remembered seeing you on television and thought if I could just talk to you, you could help me.

I knew that was impossible because I didn't know how to reach you, I didn't know anyone who could help me find you. Then some numbers came to my mind, and I scribbled them down.".
At this point she began weeping again, and I prayed silently for wisdom to help her. She continued, "I looked at the numbers and

thought, 'Wouldn't it be wonderful if I had a miracle from **GOD**, and He has given me Ken's phone number?'.

I decided to try calling it. I can't **Believe** I'm talking to you. "Are you in your office in California? "I replied, "Lady, I don't have an office in California. My office is in Yakima, Washington. "A little surprised, she asked, "Oh really, then where are you?" "Don't you know?" I responded. "You made the call." She explained, "But I don't even know what area I'm calling.

I just dialed the number that I had on this paper.". "Ma'am, you won't **Believe** this, but I'm in a phone booth in Dayton, Ohio!" "Really?" she exclaimed. "Well, what are you doing there?" I kidded her gently, "Well, I'm answering the phone. It was ringing as I walked by, so I answered it.

"Knowing this encounter could only have been arranged by **GOD**, I began to counsel the woman. As she told me of her despair and frustration, the presence of the Holy **Spirit** flooded the phone booth giving me words beyond my ability. In a matter of moments, she prayed the sinner's prayer and met the One who would lead her out of her situation into a new life.

I walked away from that telephone booth with an electrifying sense of our Heavenly Father's concern for each of His children. What were the astronomical odds of this happening? With all the millions of phones and innumerable combinations of numbers, only an all-knowing **GOD** could have caused that woman to call that number in that phone booth at that moment in time. Forgetting my drink and nearly bursting with exhilaration, I headed back to my family, wondering if they would **Believe** my story. Maybe I better not tell this, I thought, but I couldn't contain it. "Barb, you won't **Believe** this! **GOD** knows where I am!"

https://www.amazon.com/**God**s-Got-Your-Number-Gaub/dp/089221211X

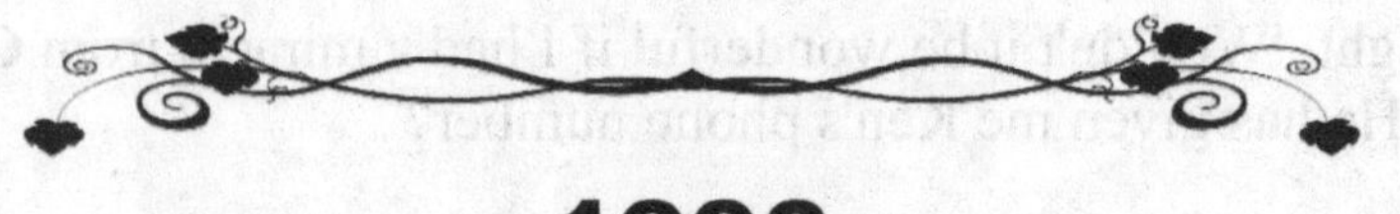

1990

Widow Lady kept calling desperate for help!

We had a precious lady in our church who was a widow. Actually I can't really say she was a member, because she would come and go. Her husband had died some years previous, leaving her behind with 2 sons and a daughter. When she 1st came into the community she had visited our church. We helped her as much as we possibly could with her moving into a rental house. She seemed to be extremely tormented and wanted or needed counselling. No matter what we said to her, it did not really seem to help.

I knew she was sincere, and was not one of those people who was **Spirit**ually, emotionally and mentally unbalanced. Now there was a major problem; once I got on the phone with her, there was no getting off. It wasn't like she was really wanting to talk, but it was like she just needed direction, and was frantically reaching out to me and other ministers to get direction. Anytime she called me, to a small extent, I would almost grit my teeth, because I knew for some strange reason I was not able to help her.

One day the phone rang, and when I picked it up, here she was wanting to speak to me. My wife was getting quite upset, not out of jealousy, but just how much time I was with her on the phone. 90% of the problem was the amount of time I was speaking on the phone with her.

This particular day that she called, we were just getting ready to sit down and eat. My wife asked me if I could get off the phone to come and eat. I asked her to give me a minute. As this precious widow lady was speaking to me, I got quiet before the Lord. I said to the Lord in my heart, **GOD** what is it that I needed to say to her? What can I even tell her?

Please listen to what I have to say, I think this is where we make a lot of mistakes, we do not really ask **GOD** what we should do. I know personally there's been many times when **GOD** spoke a warning to me, or some **Spirit**ual insight about a situation, and yet what he said to me did not really seem to help!

Now why would that be the case? It is because I did not ask him what I should do with the information he gave me. Slowly but surely I have learned that I need to stop after he speaks to me, asking him what I should do with this revelation, warning, or information!

When the enemy came to Eve in the Garden of Eden, speaking to her, she could have simply stopped him. Then she could have looked up to heaven and said: Father you hear this snake speaking to me, what should I do? If she would have done that or even her husband Adam before he ate the fruit of the tree of the knowledge of good and evil, the human race would never end up in the mess it is in.

But of course, **GOD** knew that man was not going to ask Him for direction! And this is the complexity that we find ourselves in many times! **GOD** does speak to us, but we do not follow it up by waiting on him and getting the answer.

So now here I am speaking to this widow lady, who has literally consumed many hours of my time on the phone. I had spoken all the wisdom that I knew to try to help her, but nothing seemed to help. I finally stopped! Lord what should I say to her? Up out of my belly came specific words that I was to speak.

These words were not judgmental, fault-finding or condemning. They were actually divinely inspired to encourage and to help her. I spoke these words to her. When I was done speaking these words, over the phone came joyous weeping. I literally mean that she began to weep with joy.

The question that she had been seeking did not come from me, but directly from heaven. She told me that was exactly what she needed, thanking me so much for being there to help her. She never did call me back after that, except to let me know they were moving again to another location. I wonder how many times we are spinning our tires, wasting our time and energy, striving to find an answer on our own.

We think we have biblical knowledge and that is sufficient, but what we need is a quickening of the **Holy Ghost**, and divine wisdom from the King of Kings and Lord of lords! He promised us that he would put the words that we need to speak in our mouth, in the time of need. We need to take **CHRIST** at his word! Insert chapter seven text here.

Mom cleaned because my father made her

Through the years I have tried to get my wife to be like my mom. Now I know that is extremely stupid, but I think many of us men have done the same things to our wife's if we had good mothers.

One day my wife and family and I were visiting my mother's home in Wisconsin. My mom heard me tell my wife how wonderfully organized clean the house that my mother kept. When I said this my mother just stared at me. Later that day she took me aside and she said this to me: Michael do you know why I keep our house so clean? I was a little bit befuddled by her question, and I hesitantly said no.

She said: it is because if I had not kept the house clean your father would have beat me. (I'm not adding or exaggerating anything she said to me). That's what she said! This is not to be negative towards my dad, but it is the culture that we grew up in. I never physically abused my wife, but up unto 2005 I verbally abused her. Yes I loved her deeply, but there is within us certain ideals or philosophies that must be crucified. We get it into our silly heads that our job is to transform or change people. **That is**

not our job! It is only the **Spirit** of **God** that can bring real change.

Even though my mom was threatened into a place of keeping a clean house, she was tormented all of those years. It's a terrible life to live in a home where a person is controlled and manipulated through demonic fear. May **God** deliver all of us from satanic attitudes and situations.

Albert Willis One of my Mentors

I came to know Albert because of his connection with the church I pastor called: New Covenant **Faith** Ministries! I had his son-in-law come in and speak about the tongue. Through the years brother Albert would come and minister in our church. The church he pastored was in Lafayette Louisiana.

About Elbert Willis

Reverend Elbert Willis was pastor of the Christian Center Church in Lafayette, Louisiana, and was a missionary and teacher to many nations across the world. Pastor Willis authored 66 books which have been printed in numerous languages and spread throughout the World. He had sought to bring the Gospel to the nations even up to his last days. On November 26, 2008, Reverend Willis passed away in Lafayette, La., with family at his side. Countless people across the world have been touched by his ministry and will one day walk the streets of gold with him.

Brother Albert was a man with no fear or hesitation to **Trust** the word of **God**. He is one of the few men that I knew that lived what he preached. He was very strong in a message of **Faith**, with obedience, and works that were produced because of the result of **Faith** in **Christ Jesus**.

His preaching and teaching were powerful and straightforward. He never hesitated to tell the truth even if he knew that people would be offended and would no longer support his ministry.

Albert Willis rebuked me

On one occasion I had take Brother Albert out to eat. In those days I was more than eager for people to hear what I had to say. (1990) I was speaking about soul winning, and he just sat there listening to everything I had to say.

When Albert was almost finished with eating he made a statement: **Mike I've been watching you speak about winning souls and yet I have not seen you pass out any tracks. I have not seen you share your Faith with those around us.** Then he stopped speaking, he went back to eating.

I was not offended by his correction. I simply bowed my head in shame and acknowledged that what he was saying was true. I have always tried to surround myself with people who would be bluntly honest with me. I'm not saying I invited everybody I've met to give me their opinion, because opinions like noses. **People put them what they do not belong.** But through the years I have asked people that I knew who were walking with **God** to speak correction and direction into my life.

Because I have asked specific people to speak into my life that I **Trust**, it has saved my marriage, my personal life, family life, and our ministry. **Believe** me I have only given a small handful of people that privilege, because most people I meet are not very deep in their maturity with **Christ**.

Why Albert stopped moving in the gifts

On another occasion brother Albert and I were once again at a restaurant. We began to talk about the moving's and the gifting's of the **Holy Ghost**. I informed him that I did not move in the gifts like I used to in my younger years. (Of course, at this time I was still in my 30s, but I had begun to move in the gifts of the **Spirit** right after my salvation when I was 19 years old).

That's when Albert informed me that he no longer moved in the gifts either. I asked him why was this the case? He said because when he would be teaching and preaching the word, he perceived that the people wanted him to hurry up and get done so that he would move in the gifts of the **Spirit**. Albert told me that he would operate in the word of knowledge, wisdom, gifts of healing and miracles. It got to the point where he felt like he was just performing for them. Like they really did not want the word of **God**, just miracles.

I said Elbert I think we are missing **God**. **God** knew that people would put a demand on us for signs and wonders, and yet that's exactly what the **Holy Ghost** will do. **God** confirms his word with miraculous manifestations. The full gospel is not just the preaching of the word, but that word being confirmed with signs and wonders following. Albert did not deny this reality, and you could tell he was thinking deeply about what I had said.

From that time to this I have continued to move in the gifts of the **Spirit** as **God** directs. Most of my books are filled with the supernatural manifestations of **God's Holy Ghost**. Without those supernatural experiences I would have very little testimonies. The Book of Acts is all about the acts of the **Holy Ghost**. The **Holy Ghost** is still upon the earth, wanting to confirm **God's** word with signs and wonders, miracles and supernatural manifestations. Who are we to hinder what **God** wants to do?

MY SON Danny's dyslexia

My son Daniel in his younger years had dyslexia. He writes about it in his bio for his books. (At the writing of this book 2020).

He is now completely healed from this condition supernaturally. Up to this moment he and our daughter has authored six **Christian** books. These books are averaging 400 to 600 pages. It's amazing what **God** can do when we look to him.

ABOUT THE AUTHORS

Daniel J Yeager was born dyslexic. As he grew up, many words appeared backward to him, which made it hard for him to read or write until he was eighteen and **God** miraculously healed him.

Since then, he has read hundreds of books, becoming engrossed with the art of storytelling. He and his brothers frequently stayed up late into the night, telling each other stories and passing back and forth ideas. After getting married to his wonderful wife, Yu Catherine Li, he was inspired to sit down and write out those stories. He has now written over six books.

This book was originally meant to be a short story, but the characters became alive and took on a life of their own. Now they are telling their story through him.

***

Stephanie J Yeager is a passionate singer-songwriter who turned her love of writing music into writing fantastical stories. Raised in a large family with three older brothers and a younger sister (who is now deceased), she is well versed in the make-

Believe, just ask her brother Daniel who used to tell her wild tales of Rex the dinosaur and give her rides on his back.

Now that "Rex" has become too old to carry her anymore, Stephanie now helps Daniel mentally lift people out of the mundane and into the realm of mythical creatures and wondrous secrets. With **God** as her leader and her two cats Oliver and Skyler at her tail (constantly), join her as she weaves tales of romance, excitement, battle, and miraculous, divine intervention.

Kathleen Does a CHRISTMAS Album 1990

My wife Kathee had always loved **Christ**mas as far as I know. She would even start singing **Christ**mas songs in July. She loved **Christ**mas so much that she took well-known beloved secular **Christ**mas songs and put **Christian** lyrics to them.

My children growing up heard my wife sing these songs with **Christian** lyrics. I'm not even sure if they know what the original secular songs say. Back in 1990 she told me that she wanted to do a **Christ**mas **Christian** album with the secular songs that she had changed.

I encouraged her to do it. Through a friend of ours who was our radio station engineer put us in touch with the recording studio in Hagerstown Maryland. The gentleman who ran this recording studio in Hagerstown was Mike Sokol.

He gave us instructions and how we could go about doing this legally. My wife contacted all of the different recording studios where she needed to get permission to use their background music. I cannot remember but I know that we paid to use this copyrighted material.

Dr. Michael H Yeager

My wife's Christmas album from 1990
The Heart of Christmas by Kathleen M Yeager

There was a total of 12 songs that were on the cassette. To this day that **Christ**mas album is my favorite **Christ**mas selection. The names of the songs are #1, Blessed **Christmas** (White **Christmas**) #2 **Jesus** Savior Lord and King (Winter Wonderland) #3 Silent Night - in German #4 **Jesus** Loves Me #5 awaiting a manger #6 How I Wish I Could've Been There #7 Come All Ye **Faith**ful #8 The Gift Goes on #9 **Jesus Christ** (Oh **Christ**mas Tree) #10 Little Town of Bethlehem #11 Golden Bells (Silver Bells) #12 Have Yourself a Merry Little **Christmas**

CHAPTER EIGHT

Steven's Eyes Bulging

Steven my third son was always a funny little guy. When we sat down to eat he always felt like he was not going to get his share the food. He might've got that from his dad, but I'm not quite sure. Who is his dad? Of course I am the author of this book in this biography.

I can still remember to this day as we would sit at the table. Sometimes there is something that he really liked, and he couldn't get enough of it. I wish I would've had a camera because he looked like a little chipmunk with his cheeks completely fall. He be shoving the food and so fast that I thought he would choke.

I still remember his cheeks all puffed out, with his eyes bulging. That image will be forever burned in my brain. If I would have had any wisdom I could've easily prevented his fear of not getting enough food. I should've divided the food up equally among the kids. But as they say in the world: it is what it is!

Dr. Michael H Yeager

Do You Want Some More Cookies?

Periodically I would take the children out to have pizza at Pizza Hut. I would order two large pizzas with extra toppings. My children were just extremely aggressive when it came to pizza. It was usually Fridays when we would take them out for this special meal.

One day a brilliant idea came into my head. I thought how can I stop them from eating all of the pizza and me not getting what I wanted? I went to a local grocery store and bought the biggest big of cookies I could find. Then I went home and told my family we were going to go for a ride.

We all got into our caravan, and as I was driving, I asked them if they were hungry? They told me that they were. My wife was sitting in the passenger seat but she didn't know what I was going to do. I took that big bag of cookies and handed it back to my kids. I told them: **enjoy yourself, eat all you want**. Man, did they devour all of those cookies or what! I just get driving around until every cookie was gone. Their bellies were so full that they had no more room to eat.

That's when I headed to Pizza Hut. As we pulled into the Pizza Hut restaurant, they all looked at me with tremendous suspicion in their eyes. I told them: **let's go get some pizza**. All of the kids moaned. As I ordered two large pizzas I could see that they were not going be able to eat very much. It's a wonder that none of them got sick.

When the pizzas finally arrived they tried to eat some, but they had no room in their bellies. I had a wonderful time eating all of the pizza that I wanted that day. I felt bad, and yet it was wonderful. Of course you know that this trick never worked again. I would try it periodically through the years. I would hand them a bag of cookies and tell them to enjoy them. But they never would touch those cookies. To this day it is one of the running jokes of my family. Every time I asked them if they want to have a bag of cookies they all moan remembering that day at Pizza Hut.

$500,000.00 Digital Equipment for $500.00

Because of the **Christian** school I was allowed to go purchase government surplus. One day as I was walking through one of the government facilities I came across two big machines. Each machine was designed to do digital recording for video. In 1990 that was a big deal. They wanted $250 for each machine.

I did a lot of TV broadcasting in those days, and knew that I could use these machines. I called up a friend of mine by the name of Charles Wiggins out of Ohio. I told him about these machines that I was looking at. He asked me: what do they want for them? When I told him the price he could hardly **Believe** it. Mike he said: those machines brand-new run $250,000 each. I said what? He said they cost $250,000 each brand-new. I purchased both of those machines for $500.

I was not allowed to sell them for at least a year and 1/2. Actually I never did sell them, but I traded them in for some other equipment for broadcasting. I would still have access as of 2020 for government surplus, but I stopped doing that many years ago.

Jerry Foreman Leaves Baker to Work For us

We were in the midst of updating all of our equipment, plus we were getting ready to do broadcasting by satellite. I desperately needed an engineer who knew about all this technology.

Now, I was broadcasting from channel 49 out of York Pennsylvania, and channel 68 out of Hagerstown Maryland. In the midst of my dealings with these TV stations I ran across an engineer by the name of Jerry Foreman.

I asked him if he would be interested in working for us part-time. It turns out that he had just come up Carolina where he had been working for Jim Baker. We negotiated how much should be paid an hour. We thought it was very reasonable, and hired him.

Jerry has been a real blessing to us through the years. One day I was speaking to him and that's when he informed me that he had been working for Jim Baker. I asked him why he left Jim? He told me that he saw the handwriting on the wall. He said there is just too many shenanigans going on, and he knew in his heart they were headed for big trouble.

He informed me that he had left just in time before everything hit the fan. There was so much conniving, backstabbing, and manipulation going on there he knew it was only a matter of time. He had to get out of there before everything really fell apart. That is how Jerry ended up working for us.

Just this year in 2020 he sent me a letter letting me know how much he had appreciated our ministry, and what we meant to him.

Kathleen's Hard to Eat Concoctions

Through the years my wife has become very creative in using leftovers. Actually that is her opinion, and not mine. I have seen her take everything that was in a refrigerator which was left over, and dump it into a large pan. She would put this on the stove and heated up.

She was sit is all down at the table with bowls and spoons. Then she would begin to dish out her concoction. It wasn't always bad, but many times it was. Now, my children were raised to eat this stuff, but it was difficult for me. Of course I have eaten a lot of disgusting stuff in other countries, but I did not expect it at home.

I got to the place to where every time my wife did this, I had an excuse to go somewhere else. The kids were okay because they were used to it but I wasn't. I would either stop at a restaurant or grocery store and buy something that I could eat. Eventually she did get away from doing this, but it took many years.

*Mafia call girl Converted by the Holy Ghost Who Was Dying

Dr. Michael H Yeager (1988)

One day I received a phone call from a woman who had visited our church. She was a very staunch Catholic, who had given her heart to **Christ**. She asked if I could possibly help them in a very difficult situation with their daughter. They began to explain to me that their daughter, who was a very beautiful woman, had at some point been caught up with the Mafia. She literally had become a call girl for the Mafia. In the mist of her wild activities with the Mafia, she had become completely cut off from the rest of her family. She had put the whole family through tremendous pain and suffering because of her activities.

The day came when out of the blue they received a phone call from her. She informed them that she had been having some difficulties with her body, and that after physical examinations, it was discovered that she had incurable cancer. She was in such bad condition that she could no longer work as a call girl.

As I listened to the mother, I could tell that her heart was filled with great distress, and yet there was an undercurrent of anger. She was very angry with her daughter and what she had put them through. Now they were calling me because she was finally at the very door of death itself. The medical world had done all they could for her, but there was no hope. I think in the mind of this young lady's parents I might come and do last rights like a Catholic priest. They were hoping if I could come over as soon as possible, because she was that close to death. At any moment she was going to step over the edge into eternity. I informed them that I would be right over, with my wife.

We live West of Gettysburg, but where they lived was approximately 22 miles east of us in a town called Hanover. I knew in my heart they simply wanted me to get her to **Pray** a **Prayer** of salvation, and then the blessings, and basically then they would say their goodbyes. I knew right away we were going to have a problem because I just do not operate that way. I know in my heart that there is nothing impossible with **God**, and he likes to take the most difficult situations, turn them around because of his great love, and because of who HE is.

When we arrived at the house the mother and **Father**, brothers, relatives were waiting. It felt like a funeral home. They were expecting her to die at any moment. Everything was arranged for her death! They informed us that she was nothing but skin and bones. She was excreting black and ugly fluids from her mouth, and her private parts. They just wanted me to realize that her life on earth was over. Basically, what they were saying is just **Pray** with her to bury her, making sure that she would never go back into her old lifestyle. What I am sharing with you is not me being critical of them, just knowing exactly in my heart what they were saying. Their hearts were filled with great fear that if **God** raised her up off the bed of death, she would go back to her old lifestyle.

They lived in an old two-story house, and their daughter was in a bedroom on the 2nd floor. As they were sharing with me their concerns, desires, and exactly what they wanted me to do I simply listened. I did not make any kind of statement or commitments to them, promises or insinuations of what I would do. I had not come to please them, but to hear from heaven for this young lady. I thanked them for all their information letting them know that now I would like to see their daughter.

My wife and I walked up the stairs, turned down the hallway, and went to the room they told us she was in. We knocked softly

1st, and not hearing a response, we entered. There she was, a dark-haired, at one time, a beautiful 26-year-old girl. She was lying in her bed with her eyes deep sunk but wide open. The terrible smell of death was in the room. There was a sheet covering her body, but it was easy to tell that she was nothing but skin and bones. I introduced myself with my wife, telling her that I was a pastor and we had come to **Pray** for her. It turns out that she was quite alert and responsive.

The very first thing I did was share with her the reality of **Christ** and the difference he had made in my life. At one time I had lived a very unseemly and wicked existence. I had ran with a gang outside of Chicago and done things that I was extremely ashamed of, but I had been forgiven through the precious blood of **Jesus Christ**. Now **Christ** himself lived within me, having transformed and made me into a brand-new person.

My wife also spoke for a while to her, talking softly and tenderly about the love of **Christ**. I perceive the spirit of **God** was working on her for her eyes filled with tears. We asked her if she would like to commit her heart and her life to **Jesus Christ**. And with a whisper, she said yes.

We immediately had a witness within our hearts that she truly did accept **Christ** as her Lord and Saviour and that she was now born again. Now at this point I had a choice to make; was I going to let her die and go home to be with **Jesus**, or would I share with her the reality that **Christ** could raise her from the bed of death? I could not walk away from her without telling her that **Christ** would make her whole. My wife and I began to share the truth that **Jesus** is the great physician. In his earthly life, he had healed everybody because it is **God**'s will for all to be saved and to be healed.

As I began to speak the truth of divine healing, and that by the stripes of **Jesus** we are made whole, I perceived that **Faith** was flooding into her soul. We asked her if she would allow us to ask **God** to raise her up off the bed of death. She wholeheartedly agreed with that request. We laid our hands on her in the mighty name of **Jesus Christ** of Nazareth, we commanded the spirit of cancer and death to come out of her. We commanded her bodily organs to be restored and to be made whole.

The room was filled with a wonderful sweet presence of **Jesus Christ**. After we had **Prayed** for her we encouraged her to begin to feed herself the truth of **God**'s word. We encouraged her to feed herself by good **God**ly ministers on the TV (there is one in her room) that would teach and preach Divine healing. We gave her a list of certain ministers that we knew who was on TV who strongly and boldly declares that healing is for today and for everyone.

We also informed her that we would be back as much as possible to continue to speak life over her. We would also be bringing teaching materials and cassette tapes that would encourage her in her **Faith** in **Christ**. Before we left the room, my wife and I perceived that there was already a wonderful improvement in her body. When we entered the room it had the smell of death, but now the very presence of **God**, almost a divine light, had entered the room. We told her goodbye, letting her know that we would be back soon.

My wife and I went downstairs to see the family. As we came down the stairs they were all looking up at us, wanting to know what had happened. I informed them with great joy that she had given her heart to **Christ**. I also informed them that we had **Prayed** for her to be raised up from the bed of death.

The minute I told them this, I sensed hatred coming from them towards my wife and I for **Praying** and **Believing God** for her healing. They truly did not want her to be raised up, because they really thought that she would go back to being a call girl for the Mafia. From that point forward there was great animosity in them against us. Every time we would come to their house, we could tell that they did not want us there. Often, they would not even speak to us as we came to see their daughter.

My wife and I began to visit two or three times every week. She immediately began to get better. She was eating, sitting up, and talking more. Her countenance was completely different. When we would visit her we would discuss the different biblical principles. She would tell us the ministers that she was watching and how exciting the word of **God** was. In her bedroom, there was the presence of heaven. Downstairs in the midst of her family was the presence of hell. She told us that she knew her parents were extremely upset with us because we were standing with her for her complete healing.

One Sunday morning, we were pleasantly surprised as she walked into our church underneath her strength. Yes, there were still some symptoms of cancer in her, but she was doing better every day. About two weeks after her visit, we went to see her at her parents' house. When we walked into the house, the atmosphere was not just anger, but there was also once again the sense of death hanging in the air.

I hate to say this, but they almost reminded me of vultures hanging over some animal who had just been hit on the road, waiting for the animal to die. They did not say much to us, so we simply went up the stairs. When we entered this precious sister's room, we were shocked to see her lying in her bed, with death once again hanging over the top of her. We asked her what was going on.

She informed us that it would be best for her to die because her parents and family members were so tormented over the thought that she might go back to her old lifestyle. Day by day, they had been fighting her, attacking her, and nagging her. My wife and I looked at each other, and we knew what we had to do. I told her that we had a spare bedroom in our house, and that we would gladly take her in.

We would stand with her in **Faith** until she was completely restored. And we would disciple her in the things of **God**. She thanked us with all the sincerity of our heart but told us that she could not do this. She informed us that her family already hated us for encouraging her to live, and that if we took her into our house, there would be such hatred in their hearts that they would never forgive us. She basically said goodbye to us right then and there. Our hearts were filled with great sorrow as we hugged her and as we said our last goodbyes. That was the last time we saw her alive.

It wasn't very long before she had passed on to eternity. They did ask me to do the funeral, but there was still great animosity in the air even in that service. I tried to speak as much love and comfort that I could to these tormented people, who had allowed the devil to take them captive in their thoughts and emotions. They did not **Believe** that **Christ** was big enough to transform the heart of their daughter.

What is so sad is they did not see that she had literally become a new creation. Love emanated from her for **God** and for people. The girl we had gone to visit had literally died on that first visit. **God** had raised up a new person, a brand-new creation, but those who were close to her could not see it. Our hearts were sad over the fact that she passed on, yet we rejoice that we will see her again on the other side. Not as a call girl for the Mafia, but a brand-new creation, a glorious holy, and wonderful woman of **God**.

Two fingers Stephanie

My daughter Stephanie was born on my birthday. 18th, 1988. She was such a little cutie when she was small. Actually, she still is very pretty, and a very accomplished woman.

When she was real little she used to have this favorite blanket that was white with pastel colors. She to this day she still has remnants of that blanket (she is 32 at the writing of this book).

My Amazing Journey - Doc Yeager

When she was real little she got into the habit of sticking two fingers into her little mouth. And from that habit that she had she became known to me as: **Two Fingers Stephanie**.

Another little interesting story. One day as I came through the front door of our house, Stephanie who was about two years old was coming down the stairs. The minute that she saw me, she cried out Daddy! With that declaration she launched herself into the air towards me. I had to run forward to catch her. She had taken a leap of **Faith** without thinking about getting hurt. She knew in her heart instinctively that her Daddy would be there to catch her. I think that's a tremendous illustration of what our relationship with with our heavenly father should be.

We also had another nickname for Stephanie which was after the Egyptian name they had given to Joseph the 11th son of Jacob. They called him Zaphnath-Paaneah. Stephanie's name to this day is **Stephanathaneah**.

Broadcasting On Satellite & Multiple TV Stations

In 1983 is the very first time I one on TV. I started on a little TV station out of Hagerstown which was channel 25. From there I went to channel 49 in redline PA, and channel 68 in Hagerstown Maryland. I also went on a TV station in toss Oklahoma. We eventually went on quite a number of low-power TV stations.

Eventually I was ordained by Dr. Lester Sumrall. He had a

satellite broadcasting network called: LeSEA (Lester Sumrall Evangelistic Association) I ended up broadcasting on Sumrall's satellite network five days a week with 1/2 an hour program.

Lester Sumrall, with the help and support of his family and many friends, founded the LeSEA (Lester Sumrall Evangelistic Association) in 1957: A ministry which has subsequently given birth to well over one hundred books and study guides, eleven television stations, a satellite ministry, three FM radio stations, five shortwave stations reaching over ninety percent of the world's population, and a quarterly magazine.

In 2018, LeSEA Broadcasting changed its name to Family Broadcasting Corporation (FBC). Perhaps the crowning glory of Lester Sumrall's work is his ongoing ministry to feed desperately poor families within the Body of Christ. Established in 1987, LeSEA Global Feed the Hungry® has given millions of dollars to countless Believers around the globe.

To the Rescue on a Snowmobile
KNEE SEVERLY DAMAGED!

The knee is made up of four components: bones, cartilage, ligaments, tendon. Every part of my knee severely damaged! (1992)

Mike to the rescue, or so I thought. I dressed up in all my winter trappings. I then went out and brushed the snow off my John Dear snowmobile and laid my hands on it, commanding it not to give me any problems. I should have prayed over myself first.

I started the old machine up, revving the throttle as I headed out of the church parking lot. I turned to my right going down the deserted, main highway. There I was, having the time of my life and doing it for the fire department! Here I was doing about 50 miles an hour or faster when I hit a section that was nothing but black ice.

The snowmobile's back end spun to the right out of control. I went flying through the air as it threw me for a lopper. I slammed my right kneecap extremely hard on the asphalt road. I felt my kneecap rip, break and tear as I kept sliding down the road for quite a distance. The snowmobile had continued on its way, spinning out of control.

The snowmobile itself eventually stopped because my hand was no longer cranking the throttle. Fortunately, it was not damaged because there was nothing but snow in every direction. There I was, lying in the dark on the ice-covered road in the snow and freezing wind, clutching my busted up knee, alone and in tremendous pain! It felt like blood was running down my leg. Immediately, I cried out to **JESUS** and repented for being so stupid and for not using **God**ly wisdom.

My theology is that almost everything that goes wrong in my life is usually my own stupid fault. Even if the devil is involved in it, it is most likely because I first opened the door for him. After I was done repenting and confessing to the Lord, I went aggressively after my healing.

I commanded my kneecap to be put back into its normal condition in the name of **JESUS CHRIST** of Nazareth. I commanded every broken part of my kneecap to be made whole. You see, I could grab my patella and move it all around. It was no longer attached to my knee. It seemed to have become completely disconnected, no longer restrained by its associated ligaments.

Probably at this juncture, 99.9% of people would have called it quits when it comes to completing the mission they set out on. But that is not my mode of operation. If I declared that I was healed then I needed to act upon it. I discovered a truth a long time ago, **GOD** cannot lie!

Numbers 23:19GOD is not a man, that he should lie; neither the son of man, that he should repent: hath he said, and shall he not do it? or hath he spoken, and shall he not make it good?

But let me say this; I had been hiding **GOD**s WORD in my Heart! So, I slowly crawled back over to my snow machine and pulled myself back into the seat. I painfully swung my left leg over the seat into its proper position. At that very moment, wave after wave of pain overwhelmed me.

Years of experience walking in **Faith**, however, caused me to declare that I am healed in the name of **JESUS**. In the name of **JESUS**, I am healed. Over and over I kept saying this to myself all along this painful journey! I opened the throttle and proceeded on the way to pick up the equipment operator. I kept proclaiming the truth.

On the way, there were a lot of areas where my snowmobile just would not go. The snow was way too deep in some areas to go or the road was flooded with water in others. The storm had dumped a combination of rain, ice, and snow. One would need a boat to go through some of the areas where I went. Admittedly, at times I took chances that I should not have taken. I would accelerate to high speed and just zip across the flooded areas.

The back end of the snowmobile would begin to sink as if I wasn't going to make it. But, I would constantly revert back to the old **Trust**ed declaration: In the name of **JESUS**, in the name of **JESUS**, in the name of **JESUS**, I will make it. There are a lot of wonderful messages preached on **Faith** but that's not what wins the victory. It is when the Word has been quickened in your heart that you know, that you know, that you know, that you know that **GOD** and His Word are true.

I cannot describe to you enough the immense pain and agony that I was going through, yet I did not merely think that I was healed, I knew that I was healed! **Faith** is not thinking, hoping, or wishing. It is knowing that you know, that you know, that you know. About 45 minutes later I finally reached my first destination which was a miracle!

The township worker saw me pull up outside of his house. As he came to the machine, he could not see my face because of my helmet and my ski mask. I did not tell him that I had an accident and shattered my kneecap.

I do not adhere to bragging about the devil or his shenanigans, lies or deceptions. This was no little man that I had to carry on the back of my machine either. He must have been over six feet tall, and heavy set. He mounted up and we were on our way. It took major **Faith** to keep ongoing.

We had to take numerous detours before I finally got him to the big earthmover that he was tasked to operate. He jumped off my snowmobile and thanked me for the ride. I told him it was no problem as I opened up the throttle and headed home.

This time, I decided to take a different route because the last route was so bad. It took all the **Faith** that I could muster to get back to the parsonage. I was cold, wet, tired and completely overwhelmed with pain from the shattered knee. When I got home, I just kept thanking **GOD** that I was healed. During the next couple of days, I refused to pamper my leg. I did not put any ice or heat upon it.

I did not take any kind of medication or painkillers. I did not call anyone asking them to please pray for me and to **Believe GOD** for my healing. I know this may seem extremely stupid, but I knew in my heart that I was healed. It has got to be in your heart! My head, my body, and my throbbing, busted kneecap were all telling me that I was not healed, but let **God's** Word be true and every symptom a lie.

When the next Sunday rolled around, the roads were clear enough for people to make it to church. During that time, you might have called me Hop-Along Cassidy because of the way that I was walking. I do not deny the problem, but I sure as heaven denied the right for it to exist! One of our parishioners, who was a nurse, saw me limping badly. She asked me what happened and I told her. She informed me that this was a major problem. She tried to explain to me in medical terms exactly what she thought I had done to my knee.

Medically, in order to reattach and repair my patella, I would have to endure at least one major surgical procedure. She recounted to me that she had once had a similar injury although it was nowhere near as bad as mine. She went on to elaborate that even after extensive operations, her knee was still giving her major problems. I thanked her for this information and went back to **Trust**ing and believing that by the stripes of **JESUS CHRIST,** I was healed.

I sure as heaven was not going to let go or to give up on **God's** promises. I wrestled with this situation day after day, commanding my knee to be to function as **GOD** had designed it to do. Thanking **GOD** over and over I was Healed!

When the pain would overwhelm me, I would tell it to shut up, be quiet and work! When it seemed like my leg would not carry me, I would command it to be strong in the name of **JESUS**.

This went on for well over a month. One morning I crawled out of bed and my knee cap was perfectly healed. You would think that when the healing manifested that I would begin to sing, shout and dance, but I did not and I do not! You see I had already done all of my rejoicings in advance because I **Believe** that the minute I prayed, I received! That was over 25 years ago and I am still healed!

19 GOD is not a man, that He should lie; neither the son of man that he should repent: hath He said, and shall He not do it? or hath He spoken, and shall He not make it good? Num 23:19

CHAPTER NINE

HEALED from TMJ After I Slapped her

One day a young woman came into our church who I had never seen before. When I finished ministering the Word, I gave an altar call for anybody who needed healing. In this service the **Spirit** of **GOD** was Moving Mightily in me!

Ezekiel 47:1 Afterward he brought me again unto the door of the house; and, behold, waters issued out from under the threshold of the house eastward: for the forefront of the house stood toward the east, and the waters came down from under from the right side of the house, at the south side of the altar.2 Then brought he me out of the way of the gate northward, and led me about the way without unto the utter gate by the way that looketh eastward; and, behold, there ran out waters on the right side.3 And when the man that had the line in his hand went forth eastward, he measured a thousand cubits, and he brought me through the waters; the waters were to the ankles.4 Again he measured a thousand, and brought me through the waters; the waters were to the knees. Again he measured a thousand, and brought me through; the waters were to the loins.5 Afterward he measured a thousand; and it was a river that I could not pass over: for the waters were risen, waters to swim in, a river that could not be passed over.

There have been times when I was completely swept away

by the river of the spirit. When I enter this world, it is almost like I have no control. Just like as if you swam into the middle a fast-moving river. It takes you away. This is where I found myself in this service. Many people came forward to be prayed for including this visiting woman.

Now I NEVER put Pressure upon people's heads to get them to fall. At times, through the years I do not even touch them, I simply stand in front of them and speak the Word of the Lord. The Power of **GOD** comes upon them, and they go down under the power of God!

When I came to her, I perceived by the Word of Knowledge that she had something wrong with her jaw.

(Temporomandibular disorders (TMD) occur as a result of problems with the jaw, jaw joint (or TMJ), and surrounding facial muscles)

I was so deep in the **Spirit** that before I knew what I was doing, I pulled back my right hand and I slapped her face very hard. I hit her so hard that the sound could be heard throughout our sanctuary! The congregation literally made a sound of surprise! I had never done anything like this before. I hit her so hard in the natural that there would be welts on her face!

You might say: pastor Mike I do not agree with this kind of activity. And I would say: I would completely agree with your attitude. The only problem was that I was completely taken up by the spirit of God.

The power of **GOD** hit her at that moment, and she fell out under the power of the **Spirit**. I continued to work my way down the prayer line moving in the **Spirit**. Many times, it is not until after I finish ministering that I think back to what just happened and what I did. When I minister to people and a prayer line I am not in a hurry to get to the end. During these times the Lord will give me prophetic words, mingled with words of knowledge and wisdom and discerning of spirits. It could have been anywhere from 20 minutes to 30 minutes later I finally got to the end of the line. Now When I got to the end of the line I realizedwith great trembling that I had hit this visiting young woman very hard in the face.

As I looked back over the prayer line, I noticed she was standing up. I could see that tears were rolling down her face. she was about 50 feet away from me. The right side of her face was towards me, but I could not see if there were any marks on the left side of her face where I had slapped her. I was quite concerned about what I had done.

For a while I tried to avoid her, but finally I took a deep breath and walked back across the sanctuary to my right and walked over to where she was standing. When I came in front of her, I looked at the left side of her face intently. To my utter amazement there was not one finger mark on her cheek. As hard as I had hit her with my right hand, every one of my fingerprints definitely should have been outlined on her cheek.

She was still standing there crying softly. I very gently asked her what happened. She told me that she had an illness in her face and jaw, but now she was completely healed. I asked her out of curiosity if it hurt when I slapped her.

She replied in almost an offended way, **"You slapped me?"** Embarrassed, I rephrased my question. "When I touched your face, what happened?" She said it was like a feather brushing her cheek. The power of **GOD** flooded her jaw, and she was healed. She went on her way completely healed of TMJ.

1991

Kathleens Prayer caused 40 Day Fast

How not to end a 40 day fast
(1994)

I had began to grow a little bit cold and lukewarm in my **Spirit**ual walk with **GOD**. I still was very much active in the church but I wasn't flowing in the **Holy Ghost** as I was accustomed. My wife became very concerned about me. Unbeknownst to me, she began to pray and intercede on my behalf.

Kathee's Perspective:

My heart yearned for the man I married. Michael was not on fire for **GOD** like he once was. He had become burdened by the woes and cares of life and the church. He was miserable and making us all miserable with him! My prayer to **GOD** was to bring back the man I had married and to light the fire for **GOD** that once burned bright and strong. I began anointing everything that Mike touched with oil: his truck, his clothes, even his computer. However, my prayers did not appear to be very effective; that is, until the day the **Spirit** of **GOD** came upon me! A supernatural **Spirit** of travail overtook me. This time as I prayed, I anointed his pillows and possessions with my tears instead of oil. I had truly touched heaven because that very night when Mike returned home, **GOD** was waiting for him!

Back to Michael :

When I came home from church, Kathee was already in bed asleep. I slipped out of my clothes and crawled into bed. The minute I laid my head upon my pillow, the overwhelming power of **God's** conviction hit me. It didn't seem fair! Kathee was sleeping peacefully but I was about to lose not only my sleep but so much more!

Immediately, I began to weep and cry. The conviction of **GOD** so overwhelmed me that I had to get up out of bed and begin to pray. I prayed all night long with this **Spirit** of conviction. I kept praying through the next whole day. It was so strong upon me that I was not able to stop.

Not only could I not stop praying but I had no desire for physical food. It wasn't as if I had decided not to eat, it was because I could not eat. The only thing that I could do was drink water and pray. This went on one whole day. After the first day, it did not lift but instead it increased. I went two days, then three. This continued for the next forty days and nights. Yes for the next 40 days I prayed and fasted.

I do not want to lead you to **Believe** that I did not drive my car, preach in the pulpit, check the mail or do all of the daily, mundane tasks required of all of us; I did all of those things. However, the **Spirit** of **GOD** was on me in a mighty way.

Now this was the first time that I had ever gone 40 days with drinking nothing but water. On the 41st day, I did something that was so stupid that it's hard for me to even fathom that I did it. I did not consult anyone or ask my wife. I went to the kitchen early in the morning, scrounging through the refrigerator. I was so famished; I could hardly stand it. I began to pull all kinds of things out of the refrigerator: potatoes, fruits, almost anything that I could get my hands on, including a steak. Yes, that's right, a steak! No way, Pastor Mike, you could never ever be that stupid! Oh yes, I was!

I literally devoured all that food in a very short period. It felt wonderful for less than half of an hour and then it hit me like a gigantic avalanche of overwhelming pain. I fell to the ground almost like a dead man. I felt my heart stop. I mean it literally stopped beating at times. I was a dead man because of my stupidity.

After 40 days of fasting and experiencing a divine move of the **Spirit** upon my heart, one would think that I knew better. But the old flesh was not dead. I ended up lusting for food, being consumed by a ravenous hunger. I gave into it and devoured all before me just like the children of Israel must have done when **GOD** sent them quail to eat. I wanted meat and I got it. Boy, did I ever!

To this day, I remember lying on the floor, crying out for **God's** mercy, asking him to spare my sorry life. You cannot imagine how I felt as I fought for my life just because of my stupidity. In my mind, I could imagine the headline news: *Local pastor kills himself by gorging upon food after a 40 day fast.* That sure would bring glory to **GOD** —NOT! Did I live? Obviously, but by the grace of **GOD**! I am writing this story today in order to encourage you; never break a 40 day fast by gorging yourself.

Thank **GOD** for his mercy. I can imagine **GOD** the Father, the Son, the **Holy Ghost** and all the angelic host looking down at me, shaking their heads back and forth saying, "Can he really be that stupid?!" Yup, I sure was. But thanks be to the **GOD** and Father of my Lord **JESUS CHRIST** who spared my life for another day on this little green Earth!

1 Corinthians 6:12   All things are lawful unto me, but all things are not expedient: all things are lawful for me, but I will not be brought under the power of any. 13 Meats for the belly, and the belly for meats: but GOD shall destroy both it and them. Now the body is not for fornication, but for the Lord; and the Lord for the body.

Rolex Idolatry

We once had a prophet come to church for a number of services. On the day he was to leave our fellowship, he requested to speak to me about something personal. We went into the sanctuary which was now empty of people.

As I was standing there, he removed a watch from his wrist and very timidly extended it towards me. I asked what he was doing. He told me that it was his Rolex watch and that the Lord had instructed him to give it to me. Now, I had never met this prophet before these meetings. In other words, I was a complete stranger to him. I told him that I did not want his five-thousand-dollar watch. (He informed me that that was what it was valued at.)

He insisted that he had no choice but to give it to me. He did not seem extremely enthused about this. I got quiet before the Lord, asking Him in my heart what this was about. The **Spirit** of **GOD** spoke to my heart and told me that this man was in bondage to his watch and that he needed to be set free. The only way that he would be free from this idolatry was to give the watch away. The Lord spoke to me very forcefully to relieve him of it.

I said "Okay, I will take your watch. The Lord just spoke to my heart and said that you are in bondage to it and that you need to be set free!" He did not deny nor argue with what I had just told him. He handed me the watch with a very depressed look, turned and walked out the door of our church. I really did not want this watch. You see, I'm just not into jewelry or extravagant living. I never have been and never want to be.

I contacted a local jeweler to try to sell it. I was going to use the money to spread the gospel. I told the jeweler the make and model of the watch. Now, I do not know if the jeweler lied to me, but he told me that he could buy that same watch new for six hundred dollars. Yeah, sure. He most likely could sell that watch for ten times the amount of money than he offered for it. Because I could not find a buyer, I decided to wear it.

The first thing that I had to do was to have a link taken out of it. I put that link in the fancy box that it came in. Throughout the next year, I was extremely rough with that watch. I wore it just like I would a five dollar watch from a department store. I was doing some mechanical work and somehow, I scratched the glass. The links got all dirty and grimy. Then, in the midst of moving, I misplaced its box. I never have found it to this day.

About a year went by. One day, I was in my office and the church's phone rang. The secretary answered it. She knocked on my door to tell me that the prophet (who had given me the watch) was on the line and wanted to speak to me. The last time I had heard from him was when he had given me the watch one year before. I asked the Lord what it was that he wanted. The **Spirit** spoke to my heart and said the man wanted his watch back. The Lord further said that he was still in bondage to it and he was going to ask me to sell it back to him for five hundred dollars.

I picked up my phone and for a while we went back and forth with small talk. I finally asked him what I could do for him. He asked if I still had the watch that he had given to me. I replied that I still had it. He then informed me that for the last year, he had been looking high and low for a watch just like the one he had given me but was unable to find one. He asked if I would be willing to sell it back to him.

I told him that I would not sell it but, if he wanted, he could make a donation to the church, and I would gladly send it back to him. He asked me how much of a donation I wanted. I told him that he would have to decide. After a couple of minutes, he asked me if five hundred dollars was acceptable. I told him that would be just fine. I then packed up the idol and sent it back to him immediately.

He followed by sending the church five hundred dollars. I never heard from him again. I questioned **GOD** why he had me get involved in this situation in the first place. What was quickened to me was that the Lord knew material things held very little value to me. Consequently, I would abuse, misuse and mess up that man's precious watch. Once he got his watch back and saw the damage, he would be free from its power. In the end, he really did get set free from Rolex idolatry in a roundabout way!

> *But Godliness with contentment is great gain. For we brought nothing into this world, and it is certain we can carry nothing out. And having food and raiment let us be therewith content. But they that will be rich fall into temptation and a snare, and into many foolish and hurtful*

lusts, which drown men in destruction and perdition (1 Timothy 6:6-9).

Young Lumberton's Healing

Hello pastor Mike! I know I wrote mini testimony my healing experience 30 years ago. My name is young Lamberson. Thirty years ago we use to live in Chambersburg and attend cash town **JESUS** is Lord church. At one point I had my ears Pierced on both ears but, one ear was infected and kept on seeping and bothering me greatly.

One evening Pastor Mike said there's somebody having ear problem! So I went up to the front and he began praying for me. My ear dried out instantly. Ever since I have had no problem at all! Praise **GOD**

Revival with Sylvia Clark

Freddie Clark and his family would come to park their buses and vehicles on our property usually during the summer. From there they would launch out to local churches for ministry.

In the summer of 1991, we were having a wonderful move of **God**. Once again, the Clarks came, and as Freddy would travel to minister, Sylvia would stay behind with the little children. We asked her to minister in our revival services. She agreed, and **God** supernaturally showed up. People were pulling in off the highway and come to our facility without knowing the reason why. They come in to get gloriously saved, filled with the **Holy Ghost**.

We would then take him over to the parsonage across the parking lot and baptize them in our children above ground swimming pool. Many wonderful and amazing miracles happen during that time. They were just here in the summer of 2020 and Sylvia was Sharon with the congregation some the amazing things that we saw.

Evangelist Freddy Clark

Freddy has been operating & working in the Gifts Ministry for most of his entire life. He has traveled continuously in crusades and churches for over 50 years.

Brother Clark has a unique gift from **God**. The people he prays for have testified to genuine miracles and healings in the mighty name of **Jesus**.

Sylvia Clark

Sylvia is a woman of "presence" in word and deed and in song and appearance. She is also the mother of 11 children with amazing patience to do the job. Known for conducting revival crusades and musical concerts featuring bluegrass style gospel music, Freddy and Sylvia Clark were blessed with 11 children including 2 sets of twins, twin boys, and twin girls. Freddy and Sylvia were married on June 7, 1973.

The Family

The children sing and are gifted in musicianship. They have grown up traveling and working with their parents. Their updated ages range from 45 to 23-years-old. Their names in order are: Alan, Aaron, Adam, Ashley, Andrew, Austin, Alexander, Abraham, Avery, Aimee and Amber. After nine consecutive boys, the Clarks received the heavenly promise of twin girls.

All the children can sing in vocal harmonies and solo as well as play several instruments including rhythm guitar, harmonica, acoustic bass, electric bass, mandolin, fiddle, Banjo, drums, and dobro.

Freddy, who plays twenty instruments, gave the children lessons.

"**God** imparted musical gifts to my children," Clark said. All or part of this thirteen-member family can be seen and heard in personal appearances in some part of the Nation. It is truly a moving experience to see this group perform and minister to people in the **Spirit**.

A Reprobate and an Outlaw

One Sunday morning, the **Spirit** of **GOD** moved in a powerful way. Many people came forward to be prayed for. In the prayer line was a young evangelist who had been attending our church for some time. This morning the **Spirit** of prophecy was flowing. When I came to this young man, I laid my hands upon him, he immediately fell under the power of **GOD**. I continued to go down the line ministering to the people. When I was about three people down from him the **Spirit** of **GOD** took a hold of me. I found myself back at this man's feet. I ended up straddling him with my left foot on his right side, and my right foot on his left side.

Then I reached down and grabbed his shirt with my left hand. With my right hand I began to slap his face very hard. I must have slapped him at least five times, on both sides of his cheeks. When I was done slapping him, I went back to praying for the other people. After a brief period, the **Spirit** of **GOD** took me back to him once again. I spoke by the **Spirit** of **GOD** to him. The **Spirit** of the Lord told him, "Even as my servant has slapped your flesh, so you must slap your flesh. If you do not crucify your flesh, you will become a reprobate and a fugitive from the law!"

When the **Spirit** of **GOD** moves upon me that strong sometimes, I do not even completely remember the things that I say. After the service, I did not consider what had happened.

Three days later I received a phone call from one of the ladies in the church. She was weeping and said that her twenty some year-old daughter had ran away with this particular evangelist, and that previously he had been having a sexual relationship with another lady in our church. I prayed with her over the phone.

Approximately one month later I received another phone call from this same lady. She informed me that this man had beaten her daughter, and that they had gone out one-night drinking, when they were pulled over by a policeman. This evangelist got in an argument with the officer, which ended up with him physically fighting this policeman. Before he knew what, he was doing, he had grabbed the police officer's revolver out of his holster and aimed the gun at the cop. He then left her daughter and the police officer and ran for his life. Supposedly, he was headed for Canada. The last time I had heard, he was a fugitive of the law.

I therefore so run, not as uncertainly; so fight I, not as one that beateth the air: But I keep under my body, and bring it into subjection: lest that by any means, when I have preached to others, I myself should be a castaway (1 Corinthians 9:26-27).

CHAPTER TEN

Dome-ites of the Brain

If you come to the church's property you will see an unusual sight. On the main campus there are two geodesic dome structures. One that is 80 feet wide by 30 feet high. It is made of an aluminum frame. A large tent used to hang from the inside of it, which the minister used for storage. Heavy snow one year tore it down.

Then another smaller geodesic dome house. Across the street is a 50' x 45' fiberglass geodesic dome. There was also another dome on that property which was 80 feet wide and only about 25 feet high. This low-profile geodesic dome crumbled during a heavy snow because the foundation wasn't built correctly.

Pastor Mike also built a geodesic dome up in the mountains that was 50' x 45'. This geodesic dome to this day is used for a homeless shelter for people who need a new start in life. Two of these geodesic domes were actually built by the original creator, **Buckminster Fuller**. Buck was an ingenious inventor. The two fiberglass domes Doc Yeager built were originally owned by the military for radar systems. They were placed on 50 foot high steel towers in rough terrains like Alaska.

Richard Buckminster Fuller (July 12, 1895 – July 1, 1983)[1] was an American architect, systems theorist, author, designer, inventor, and futurist. He styled his name as R. Buckminster Fuller in his writings, publishing more than 30 books and coining or popularizing such terms as "Spaceship Earth", "Dymaxion" (e.g., Dymaxion house, Dymaxion car, Dymaxion map), "ephemeralization", "synergetics", and "tensegrity".

Fuller developed numerous inventions, mainly architectural designs, and popularized the widely known geodesic dome; carbon molecules known as fullerenes were later named by scientists for their structural and mathematical resemblance to geodesic spheres. He also served as the second World President of Mensa International from 1974 to 1983

Domeitis of the brain

Through the years many tourits have come by to look at these structures. Any time they had a chance to meet with Pastor Mike, he was asked if it was **God** that instructed him to put up all of these geodesic dome structures? His reply is: **absolutely not**. He simply got an ideal into his head and he acted upon it. That's why we should be very careful with what we allow to enter our mind. It will produce if we keep thinking on it whether we wanted to or not. Our brain is like an incubator. When you allow a thought to come, and you keep sitting on it, thinking about it, talking about it it will eventually hatch whether it be good or evil.

Proverbs 4:23 Keep thy heart with all diligence; for out of it are the issues of life.

Pamela healed of TMJ

One day as I was ministering in our church, and I was just finishing up with the message the word of the Lord came to me. I told one of the members to go get Pamela Flickinger. I Pamela was working in a children's church ministry.

When she came into the sanctuary I called her up front. I did not know this in a natural, but the word of knowledge had come to me that she had TMJ.

The temporomandibular (tem-puh-roe-man-DIB-u-lur) joint (TMJ) acts like a sliding hinge, connecting your jawbone to your skull. You have one joint on each side of your jaw. TMJ disorders — a type of temporomandibular disorder or TMD — can cause pain in your jaw joint and in the muscles that control jaw movement.

I told Pamela you have TMJ, but I'm going to pray for you, and in three days it will be completely gone, and it will never come back.

I laid my hands upon her and commanded the TMJ to go in the name of **Jesus**. After I prayed for her, she went back to this children's church. Many years later when we were talking one day she brought this situation back up to me. I had completely forgot about that day, or the prophetic word I gave her.

She told me: Pastor Mike when you called me and I had no idea what you called me for. I did have TMJ, and you prayed for me. You told me in three days it would be gone, and it was. From that moment to now (over 30 years) it has never come back.

Traveling Great Britain from Top to Bottom

I have had the wonderful experience of going to Great Britain (five times) from Wales and Scotland. I had the privilege of seeing many miracles and wonders on these five journeys.

Completely Crippled Woman Healed in England

At one meeting where I was conducting a citywide healing service, there was a very heavyset lady in a wheelchair on the front row. This meeting was not held in a church, but it was a community center so that other churches would come together.

After I was finished ministering the Word of **GOD** on the subject of healing, the **Holy Ghost** quickened me to go over and lay my hands upon this lady. I had no idea what was wrong with her. As I laid my hands upon her, I commanded her to be healed and made whole in the name of **JESUS CHRIST** of Nazareth.

When I was finished praying and commanding her to be healed, I told her to get up out of her wheelchair and walk whenever she was ready. Then I took two or three steps back away from her. I saw **Faith** flashing in her eyes! She began to push her large body up out of her wheelchair. When she was finally standing up on her feet, she began to move her feet forward one little step at a time. She was walking! It really did not seem that spectacular to me, but the congregation was amazed.

After the service, I discovered what had happened to her. She had been in a terrible car accident ten years previously, and both of her legs were extremely damaged to the point that they were useless. One leg was so mangled that the doctors had insisted on it being amputated. This precious sister refused to let them take her mangled crippled leg. She had not walked since the accident and now she was walking. Glory to **GOD**!

JESUS answered and said unto them, Go and shew John again those things which ye do hear and see: The blind receive their sight, and the lame walk, the lepers are cleansed, and the deaf hear, the dead are raised up, and the poor have the gospel preached to them (Matthew 11:4-5).

Holy Ghost Falls in Wales

A good friend of mine who has gone to be home with the Lord, (Malcolm White) use to set up my meetings in Great Britain! He had me go to a church that was not Pentecostal but did not tell me this!

I was preaching once in a very old rustic church in Wales. The church was filled with many elderly people the night I was there. I think they were celebrating eighty-nine years of ministry since the founding of the church. There were approximately thirty to forty people in the service.

These people looked to me as if they could have all been there at the founding of the church. (Maybe they did not look quite that old.) Their pastor was a young **Spirit**-filled man who I had spent the afternoon fellowshipping with. That's where I made my mistake.

Knowing that this pastor was **Spirit**-filled and excited about **JESUS**, I reasonably thought that this whole church had come into the experience of the **Holy Ghost**. I was about to find out that I was wrong! A very strong stirring of the **Spirit** gripped my heart, I preached with fire and compassion in the **Holy Ghost**.

As I was finishing the message, the **Spirit** quickened me and the word of knowledge began to flow. As I looked over the congregation, I could see what was specifically wrong in people's bodies. This does not always happen, but it is wonderful when it does.

I began to call specific people out of their chairs. They all seemed to be a little bit hesitant to come forward. I thought maybe they were simply timid. (The Welsh people tend to be that way.) I kept encouraging them to come as I called them. The first person I called was a little old lady. As she came towards me, she crumpled right to the floor about ten feet away.

This seemed to cause quite a commotion. These old men jumped up and began to hobble their way over to her. I told them that she was okay and that it was the **Spirit** of **GOD** upon her, making her whole. Then I called out another person to come forward. This man came hesitantly towards me. At about ten feet away from me, without me touching him, or waving my hands at him, he crumpled to the floor. The same old men who were trying to get this lady up divided into two groups now. One group came over to try to help the older gentleman.

As I continued to minister, more people were falling under the power. I was having a wonderful time. I was excited! **GOD** was really moving in a spectacular way in this meeting. But something seemed to be seriously wrong. After I was done ministering, it seemed like people were avoiding me like the bubonic plague. As I was getting ready to leave, I noticed that all of these old men had surrounded the young pastor.

I left the church shortly after the meeting. Someone later told me as a result of the move of the **Spirit** of **GOD** in this service, the board of that church fired the pastor. It turns out they had never seen a move of the **Spirit**. I really felt bad for this pastor being fired. I was told that the pastor had been hiding the fact that he was **Spirit**-filled because he did not want to lose the church. He eventually pastored a church that was hungry for the things of the **Spirit** of **GOD**.

Saying, What shall we do to these men? for that indeed a notable miracle hath been done by them is manifest to all them that dwell in Jerusalem; and we cannot deny it. But that it spread no further among the people, let us straitly threaten them, that they speak henceforth to no man in this name. And they called them, and commanded them not to speak at all nor teach in the name of JESUS (Acts 4:16-18)

Preaching on the streets of Great Britain

Through the years I have had the wonderful privilege of ministering in Great Britain (since about 1981). A good friend of mine who has gone home to be with the Lord, Malcolm White, used to set up my meetings. I told him that I did not want to be sitting around and wasting time.

Malcolm, I said: keep me as busy as you can. Most of these journeys were for three-week periods. I preached everywhere I had an opportunity, whether it be in the streets, churches of all denominations, old folks' homes, or in the public school system. Plus, I told Malcolm that I did not want to stay at the same church for more than one day, because I was distributing cassettes and teachings everywhere I went.

In 21 days, I would usually speak in at least 20 different locations. It was quite hectic because sometimes Malcolm had me on the train from Wales to Scotland. The next day from Scotland to England, then back to Scotland, then back to Wales. I crisscrossed over the country more times than I can remember. Sometimes the offerings were enough to cover my expenses, but that was never my concern.

To me, there is something mystical and amazing about this nation that has such a long history. Many times I have preached in the streets, including Piccadilly Square in London. I made myself available to the churches to work with them on the streets, so they would schedule outdoor meetings. In most cases they would have people who could play the guitar, and other instruments, go with me. My family and I have done this in different locations in the USA. The singing will begin to draw a crowd, and then you speak the word of **GOD** to them.

Now the problem I discovered in Great Britain is that yes we would get a nice crowd, during the singing, but they will not hang around very long as you begin to declare the word of **GOD**. One time I was ministering at a church in Bath England, where we had a wonderful service in the church facility. We had some time on our hands after the service, so they set up for me to go out into the streets.

As our singers and musicians began to sing, people began to gather. I think there was probably about 30 to 50 people standing listening, when they motioned for me to come and preach. I went up to the lead singer, telling him that we were going to do something a little bit different this time. I encouraged him and his team to just keep on singing. That the rest of the people who were with us there to evangelize would simply spread throughout the crowd sharing **CHRIST**.

They agreed to do this. Something amazing happened, as they were singing people kept coming. Before we knew it, we ended up with a massive crowd. The crowd was so large that the streets became congested. Then here came the Bobbies in the mist of this crowd. They did not interfere with the singing of our team, but simply began to direct the traffic. It was amazing because it seemed like they were working with us instead of against us.

In the mist of this massive crowd we began to speak to groups of people. I would have 3 to 5 people standing around me, some of them punkers, speaking the word to them. One of the other team members would be ministering to another group of people. It seemed like when we spoke to them one-on-one, they were more receptive to hear what we had to say. **GOD** touched many hearts that day, by the music and one on one!

We need to be flexible, and sensitive to the Holy **Spirit** when it comes to reaching the lost. If we don't, we may get caught up in a rut of how we think it needs to be done. May **CHRIST** help us to reach the lost and the hurting. The harvest is great but the laborers are few, May the Lord of the harvest send forth workers into the harvest field.

Embracing the Sufferings of CHRIST

I heard a very interesting story from another minister of the gospel. Supposedly (if I have my story correct) he was in China ministering. At the end of his service, he was having a conversation with another Chinese **Believer**. They were talking about the sufferings, persecutions, and afflictions that were taking place in China against the body of **CHRIST**. This particular man said he knew of a situation where the government had arrested a pastor. This pastor was taken to prison for quite a long time.

As he was in prison, they began to torture him, afflict him, and do terrible things to him in order that he would renounce his **Faith**. But thank **GOD**, he never did. I do not know how long this went on before he was finally released, but it was implied that it was for quite a while. When he was finally let go, he eventually made it back to the church he had pastored. He stood before his congregation sharing with them his testimony, how **GOD** had preserved him and kept him, that he had not denied the **Faith**. He also shared in detail all of the terrible things that had happened to him while he was in prison for the name of **JESUS**. All of the sufferings, tortures and pains he had endured for **JESUS CHRIST**. The entire congregation that day, all the **Believers**, broke out in weeping and crying.

When this Chinese **Believer** had finished his story, this visiting minister said, "They must've really loved their pastor." When he said this, the Chinese **Believer** looked at him oddly. He asked, what do you mean? The American minister replied, the way they were weeping and wailing and crying for him. This Chinese **Believer** said, oh no, you have it all wrong. You completely misunderstand. They were not crying because the pastor was tortured! They were weeping and crying because they felt there was something wrong with them in the fact that they had not been arrested themselves and tortured for **CHRIST**! They were literally jealous of their pastor for being so blessed in being tortured for **CHRIST**.

Acts 5:41And they departed from the presence of the council, rejoicing that they were counted worthy to suffer shame for his name.

1 Peter 4:13 But rejoice, inasmuch as ye are partakers of CHRIST's sufferings; that, when his glory shall be revealed, ye may be glad also with exceeding joy.14 If ye be reproached for the name of CHRIST, happy are ye; for the Spirit of glory and of GOD resteth upon you: on their part he is evil spoken of, but on your part he is glorified.15 But let none of you suffer as a murderer, or as a thief, or as an evildoer, or as a busybody in other men's matters.16 Yet if any man suffer as a Christian, let him not be ashamed; but let him glorify GOD on this behalf.

We as Western **Believers** seem to have no concept of what it really means to be **God's** people. I have heard from very reliable sources that the **Believers** in China really feel sad for us. They literally pray and weep for us because we are so fleshly and worldly, self-centered, self-serving, and self-seeking, because we are nothing but slaves to our emotions and to carnality.

You cannot Believe how many people, so-called Believers in America, that literally Believe we are more Spiritual and more mature than most other people in other countries. This could not be farther from the truth. GOD has allowed me to be in the midst of other Believers in poverty-stricken countries where they have nothing, yet many of them are more Spiritual mature then we are. They literally put us to shame! May GOD have mercy on our souls.

Conclusion

I have shared with you from my heart some of the experiences that the Lord has allowed me to go through. I know that what I have shared could never fully capture what took place in my journey to my time spent in heaven. But I pray that the Lord has used it to touch your life in some degree.

The harvest is truly great, but the laborers are few. I hope this book would become a catalyst that God could use to bring about a supernatural, enabling encounter with Him. If there was ever a time the body of Christ needs to be active, it is now.

"No man that warreth entangleth himself with the affairs of this life; that he may please him who hath chosen him to be a soldier"(2Tim.2:4).

You see, God is not a respecter of persons. But every one of us has a different job, a different position, a unique place within the body. Do not believe or accept the lie that God does not have a specific purpose for your life. After God created the heavens and the earth, He put in to place a new law.

God made it so that man became the gateway, channel, and avenue by which He would move, rule, and reign. There are an overwhelming amount of Scriptures that clearly proclaimed this a mazing truth. Hebrews chapter eleven reveals the names of twenty-two people God used to bring about His ultimate purpose and plan. The entire Bible is a declaration that it is now through man that God steps into the midst of humanity. God is looking and searching for men and women who will agree with His heart.

"And God blessed them, and God said unto them, Be fruitful, and multiply, and replenish the earth, and subdue it: and have dominion over the fish of the sea, and over the fowl of the air, and over every living thing that moveth upon the earth" (Gen. 1:28).

"For the prophecy came not in old time by the will of man: but holy men of God spake as they were moved by the Holy Ghost" (2 Pet. 1:21).

The heavenly Father stepped into this world through Jesus Christ to deliver, heal, save, and set men free. He was the physical embodiment of all that the heavenly Father is. He is the answer and solution to all of the world's problems.

"Neither is there salvation in any other: for there is none other name under heaven given among men, whereby we must be saved" (Acts 4:12).

Now it is our turn to be surrendered and submitted to the heavenly Father, His precious Son, and the Holy Ghost. We were made to be possessed, inhabited, filled, and under the influence of the Three in One. God has given to us the opportunity to be coworkers in the harvest field. Let us go forth in His mighty name. By His divine grace, power, authority, and His name may we go forth to set the multitudes free!

> "Remember, the most trying time is the most helpful time. In your weakness, God will make you strong."

ABOUT THE AUTHOR

Michael met and married his wonderful wife (Kathleen) in 1978. As a direct result of the Author and his wife's personal, amazing experiences with God, they have had the privilege to serve as pastors/apostles, missionaries, evangelist, broadcasters, and authors for over four decades.

They have broadcasted the Gospel on their own radio stations. Propagated the Gospel by TV, Satellite and Internet. Owning their own 24-hour TV network (wbntv.org). Having personally helped start over 27 churches.

Doc has published over 200 books, with many more coming (Lord willing). Pioneered a Bible College, and Christian school. He has thousands of video sermons on the Internet. Having written over 5000 sermon outlines on over 30 different subject matters of the Bible. Preached over 10,000 times.

Having memorized much of the New Testament! Earned a PhD in Biblical Theology, and received a conferred Doctor of Divinity from Life Christian University.

Their books are filled with literally thousands of their amazing testimonies of Gods protection, provision, healing's, miracles, and answered prayers.

Websites Connected to Doc Yeager.

www.jilmi.org

www.wbntv.org

How to Live in the Miraculous!

This is a quick explanation of how to live and move in the realm of the miraculous. Seeing divine interventions of God is not something that just spontaneously happens because you have been born-again. There are certain biblical principles and truths that must be evident in your life. This is a very basic list of some of these truths and laws:

1. You must give Jesus Christ your whole heart. You cannot be lackadaisical in this endeavour. Being lukewarm in your walk with God is repulsive to the Lord. He wants 100% commitment. Jesus gave His all, now it is our turn to give our all. He loved us 100%. Now we must love Him 100%.

My son, give me thine heart, and let thine eyes observe my ways (Proverbs 23:26).

So then because thou art lukewarm, and neither cold nor hot, I will spew thee out of my mouth (Revelation 3:16).

2. There must be a complete agreement with God's Word. We must be in harmony with the Lord in our attitude, actions, thoughts, and deeds. Whatever the Word of God declares in the New Testament is what we wholeheartedly agree with.

Can two walk together, except they be agreed? (Amos 3:3).

For the eyes of the LORD run to and fro throughout the whole earth, to shew himself strong in the behalf of them whose heart is perfect toward him (2 Chronicles 16:9).

3. Obey and do the Word from the heart, from the simplest to the most complicated request or command. No matter what

the Word says to do, do it! Here are some simple examples: Lift your hands in praise, in everything give thanks, forgive instantly, gather together with the saints, and give offerings to the Lord, and so on.

I can of mine own self do nothing: as I hear, I judge: and my judgment is just; because I seek not mine own will, but the will of the Father which hath sent me (John 5:30).

4. **Make Jesus the highest priority of your life**. Everything you do, do not do it as unto men, but do it as unto God.

If ye then be risen with Christ, seek those things which are above, where Christ sitteth on the right hand of God. Set your affection on things above, not on things on the earth (Colossians 3:1-2).

5. **Die to self! The old man says, "My will be done!"** The new man says, "God's will be done!"

I am crucified with Christ: nevertheless I live; yet not I, but Christ liveth in me: and the life which I now live in the flesh I live by the faith of the Son of God, who loved me, and gave himself for me (Galatians 2:20).

Now if we be dead with Christ, we believe that we shall also live with him (Romans 6:8).

6. **Repent the minute you get out of God's will—no matter how minor, or small the sin may seem.**

(Revelation 3:19).

As many as I love, I rebuke and chasten: be zealous therefore, and repent.

7. **Take one step at a time.** God will test you (not to do evil) to see if you will obey him. *Whatever He tells you to do: by His Word, by His Spirit, or within your conscience, do it.* He will

never tell you to do something contrary to His nature or His Word!

For whosoever shall do the will of my Father which is in heaven, the same is my brother, and sister, and mother (Matthew 12:50).

Then went he down, and dipped himself seven times in Jordan, according to the saying of the man of God: and his flesh came again like unto the flesh of a little child, and he was clean (2 Kings 5:14).

<u>Some of the Books Written by Doc Yeager:</u>

"Living in the Realm of the Miraculous – "1 to 5 "
"I need God Cause I'm Stupid"
"The Miracles of Smith Wigglesworth"
"How Faith Comes 28 WAYS"
"Horrors of Hell, Splendors of Heaven"
"The Coming Great Awakening"
"Sinners in The Hands of an Angry GOD",
"Brain Parasite Epidemic"
"My JOURNEY to HELL" - illustrated for teenagers
"Divine Revelation of Jesus Christ"
"My Daily Meditations"
"Holy Bible of JESUS CHRIST"
"War In The Heavenlies - (Chronicles of Micah)"
"My Legal Rights to Witness"
"Why We (MUST) Gather! - 30 Biblical Reasons"
"My Incredible, Supernatural, Divine Experiences"
"How GOD Leads & Guides! - 20 Ways"
"Weapons of Our Warfare"
"How You Can Be Healed"
"Hell Is For Real"
"Heaven Is For Real"
"God Still Heals"
"God Still Provides"
"God Still Protects"
"God Still Gives Dreams & Visions"
"God Still Does Miracles"
"God Still Gives Prophetic Words"

9 798352 081228